D0830448

PROTECT
YOURSELF
—— *in the* ——
HOSPITAL

**Insider Tips for Avoiding Hospital Mistakes
for Yourself or Someone You Love**

Thomas A. Sharon, R.N., M.P.H.

Contemporary Books

Chicago   New York   San Francisco   Lisbon   London   Madrid   Mexico City
Milan   New Delhi   San Juan   Seoul   Singapore   Sydney   Toronto

The *McGraw·Hill* Companies

Library of Congress Cataloging-in-Publication Data

Sharon, Thomas A.
    Protect yourself in the hospital : insider tips for avoiding hospital mistakes for yourself or someone you love / Thomas A. Sharon.—1st ed.
        p.   cm.
    ISBN 0-07-141784-2
    1. Medical errors—Prevention.   2. Hospital care—United States.   3. Iatrogenic diseases—Prevention.   4. Hospitals—Evaluation.   I. Title.

    R729.8T468   2003
    362.1′1—dc21   2003010557

1 2 3 4 5 6 7 8 9 0   AGM/AGM   2 1 0 9 8 7 6 5 4 3

ISBN 0-07-141784-2

Interior design by Scott Rattray

McGraw-Hill books are available at special quantity discounts to use as premiums and sales promotions, or for use in corporate training programs. For more information, please write to the Director of Special Sales, Professional Publishing, McGraw-Hill, Two Penn Plaza, New York, NY 10121-2298. Or contact your local bookstore.

This book is printed on acid-free paper.

Contents

Introduction

IT IS MY INTENT to educate and not to frighten people. Hospitals are a necessary part of our lives. What choice do we have if, heaven forbid, we are bleeding or suffering from a heart attack or a stroke or a fracture? Those of us who have to rush to a hospital are arriving there in a frightened, vulnerable state. Although we might complain bitterly if health-care workers ignore us, we just do not have the presence of mind to scrutinize the services they provide. Consequently, we put too much trust in doctors, nurses, and corporate management. All too often, we keep quiet even when things do not look right, for fear of antagonizing the people on whom we depend for survival.

According to a well-known Harvard University study of 1999, hospitals kill nearly 100,000 people each year because of human errors, faulty techniques, malfunctioning equipment, wanton carelessness, oversights, or criminal assaults. Many more leave the hospital worse off than when they went in. These counts are greater than the number of casualties that occur from automobile accidents on our roads and highways. Thus after reading this book, you will know how to recognize many hospital situations that are likely to cause serious injury or death.

Although not all bad outcomes are foreseeable, there are repetitive preventable calamities that occur in hospitals across the country. I have been reviewing hospital charts for malpractice attorneys all over the United States for the past eighteen years, and I have seen the same things happening repeatedly with tragic consequences to people of all ages—bedsores, fractures, nerve damage, choking, brain damage, hemorrhage, and death.

Such avoidable catastrophic mishaps occur for a variety of reasons, some of which are negligence, environmental hazards, poor judgment, personality disorders, burnout, and criminal behavior. This seems overwhelming, given that the mission statement of every hospital denotes caring and compassionate community service. We need to keep in mind, however, that we are dealing with a system of services provided by the best and the worst of human beings who are sometimes at their best and sometimes at their worst.

More specifically, there are two basic categories of avoidable disaster: acts of omission and acts of commission. The former refers to the failure to treat or correct a clinical or environmental condition that results in traumatic injury, permanent loss of organ function, or death. The latter refers to a variety of blunders that cause catastrophic or fatal injury such as dropping patients on the floor, surgical slipups, medication errors, and improper technique in performing invasive bedside procedures or physical abuse. The result is always the same—pain, anguish, grief, and terrible financial losses.

You will have the opportunity to examine the preconditions that trigger common accidents, oversights, blunders, or abuse. First, there are those injuries that are associated with being in a particular area of the hospital, such as the emergency room or operating suite. For example, a forensic expert can identify a lower leg paralysis as having resulted from a part of the operating table pressing behind the knee (peroneal nerve plexus).

Second, certain types of patients are prone to certain hospital-induced complications such as bedsores, traumatic injuries, and infections. You will come to understand the general standards of care and be able to monitor the services that hospitals provide. You will also recognize whether or not the health professionals provided prior services appropriately. Virtually all of the thousands of plaintiffs' depositions that I have reviewed revealed that patients and family members did not know that the nurses deprived the patient of necessary services such as turning and repositioning every two hours to prevent bedsores.

Third, the financial incentives of many hospitals result in executive decisions that deprive patients of access to additional technology. For example, there are new devices available to promote healing of leg ulcers in people with diabetes. Yet thousands of those individuals undergo avoidable amputation because some health-care executives refuse to purchase or rent such equipment. The information that there is a machine available offering a reasonable chance to save the leg without risk never reaches the patients.

Fourth, there is still an ongoing problem called hospital-induced anemia. This is a bizarre situation, because hospital executives and doctors have known about this problem for thirty years, it is easy to eliminate, and it perpetuates to this day. Critically ill patients are especially vulnerable. Nurses, doctors, and phlebotomists are simply drawing too much blood for laboratory tests. The victim usually suffers multiple complications leading to heart damage, brain damage, kidney failure, and death.

Fifth, current hospital staffing levels make it impossible for nurses to maintain a minimum standard of goal-oriented nursing care. Staffing levels on all shifts are so dangerously low in some places that family members need to remain at the bedside twenty-four hours per day and learn something about the patient's needs. Too many unfortunate souls are being found stone-cold dead in the hospital room, and no one has a clue as to when the victims took their last breath. Moreover, nursing supervisors spend most of their time finding nurses to fill vacant spots throughout the hospital for the next shift and have little time to monitor the quality of care.

Sixth, there are a variety of typical medication errors with a recent proliferation of narcotic overdose causing respiratory depression and death. The narcotic-related deaths and damaged brains appear to be a direct result of the development of a zero tolerance for pain program as a standard of care. This program includes the provision of a machine that allows the patient to self-administer measured doses of morphine and other narcotics intravenously or directly into the spine.

Seventh, there are certain behaviors that we can recognize as indicators that a particular patient is going to be a victim of delayed responses to calls for assistance. This happens most often to patients who are frequent complainers. They are more emotionally needy with a lower tolerance for pain and discomfort. Nurses and doctors develop disdain and contempt for such patients, labeling them as having the "cry wolf" or the "FOS" (full of shit) syndrome.

Finally, the scourge of managed care has resulted in a variety of problems including early discharge with a planned deprivation of necessary diagnostic tests and procedures. This has given rise to the patient-dumping syndrome. Many different types of injuries and complications occur in the home as a direct result of the lack of proper discharge planning. For example, hospitals often send patients home with indwelling chest catheters connecting directly to the inferior vena cava (major vein near the heart) without adequate nursing coverage. The result is sepsis (bacterial infection in the blood), accidental hemorrhage, or both.

In summary, despite the myriad of regulatory surveys at the local, state, and federal levels with visits from the Joint Commission on Accreditation of Healthcare Organizations (JCAHO) every three years, the causes of hospital-induced injury and death remain unresolved. In fact, they occur with such regularity that given any of the circumstances mentioned herein, one could virtually predict a catastrophe that is waiting to happen. Thus the malpractice continues with a staggering number of lawsuits in the judicial system. The root cause of this dilemma is the public being unaware of the fact that hospital managers enjoy an unearned public trust. Therefore, I hope that the information offered in this book will provide some insight and prompt people to question what they do not understand and insist on quality performance by experienced hands. So, the next time you see someone who looks like a teenager coming toward you with a long wide needle and quivering fingers wanting to insert it into your spine, you would do well to ask, "How many times have you done this before?"

1

Evaluating Hospital Safety: A New Rating Tool

THE HOSPITAL HAS BECOME the centerpiece of every community. It is a place where life begins and ends. It is a local center where all kinds of people turn up—billionaires, beggars, and everyone in between. They go there to receive comfort and seek a cure for their ills. Some get at least a portion of what they came for, but for many unfortunate others, that is not the case.

Every service area of the medical center has inherent perils that will produce a certain number of fatal or debilitating injuries that are specific to that part of the building and/or those types of services. This is so because there is a fault inherent in the design of our health-care systems. To comprehend the nature of this flaw, it is vital to examine the various peculiarities of the emergency room, medical or surgical floor, intensive care unit, mother-baby units, operating suite, and postanesthesia care unit (recovery room).

This concept is comparable to a product that is destined to cause damage because its intended function results in an undesired spin-off. For instance, there was a child's doll that was selling off the charts about six years ago because it had a motor mouth that simulated eating. I thought it was great. What a novel idea—we had dolls that could walk, talk, drink, and urinate. Now one could eat and chew solid plastic "food." I bought one for my youngest daughter, Isa, for her fourth birthday. She shrieked with delight when she opened the box. A few hours after she started playing with this thing, I heard her screaming. The doll morphed into a monster that had swallowed a big wad of Isa's hair and kept on chewing its way toward her scalp. We started with a toy that we thought would thrill any child for hours at a time, and we ended with a harrowing menace. Within a few weeks of our incident, Isa's doll was on the six o'clock news and the manufacturer was recalling the product. Apparently, thousands of other little girls had a similar experience. This proved that our incident was the consequence of the toy's design. The engineers' intentions were delight and happiness, and the result was pain and alarm.

Similarly, in the health-care industry, the mission is to ease suffering and save lives, but in hundreds of thousands of patients every year, we get the opposite result because of inherent design defects. This is not just random human error. If it were, we would not see the same mistakes being repeated by different people in every hospital in the country and possibly on this planet.

The commonality of consumer experience causes us to find fault with the mechanical engineering design of the hair-eating doll. Thus using the same logic, we can deduce that if people suffer the same type of injury in a particular area of a hospital in virtually every facility across the country, there must be a series of flaws in what the industry considers a time-honored standard structural design and/or accepted methodologies of delivering the services. We have already seen many generally accepted medical standards change in the face of discovering that a particular style of medical practice or a drug was actually causing harm on a large scale.

One such example was the practice of performing indiscriminate tonsillectomies on children. During the 1940s and 1950s, this procedure was almost as common as haircuts. Now we realize that the tonsils perform a vital function in our resistance to lower respiratory tract infections, so doctors are not inclined to remove these organs unless they are large enough to likely cause airway obstruction.

Another illustration of a seemingly noble intention with a bad result was the Phen-Phen and Redux craze that started as a miracle cure for obesity and ended up causing heart valve damage in thousands of consumers. Plaintiff attorneys accused the involved pharmaceutical executives of rushing to market without adequate investigation for potential side effects.

Lastly, there was the diethylstilbestrol tragedy. This drug actually stopped miscarriages and allowed pregnant mothers to carry their babies to full term. The same substance caused many of the female babies to contract a deadly uterine cancer in their early twenties—another case of noble intent turning into an unimaginable nightmare.

Being an Educated Health-Care Consumer

Given that the entire health-care system has built-in adverse effects that will continue to harm a certain percentage of consumers, the question remains "What can we do about it?" The health-care delivery system is crying out for an overhaul. Change requires motivation, but the blind trust many of us have negates the motivation for change. As long as some of us continue to have unquestioning faith in health-care providers and executives, the system will continue to produce its casualties, and the people who operate the facilities will go on referring to these recurring mishaps as "unfortunate but unavoidable."

Thus one answer lies in each of us becoming an educated consumer. Once you realize a few basic truths, you and your family members will be equipped to recognize those conditions that are unsafe and can refuse to accept them. Once the chief executive officer (CEO) of the hospital and its board of directors receive enough protests, the wheels of change are more likely to be set in motion. If no one complains, nothing changes. Additionally, as an informed patron, you can engage in consciousness-raising dialogue with health-care professionals, making them more responsive to your need for comfort, dignity, and safety.

The Overcrowded Trauma Center

A few years ago, a community hospital in a New York suburb had completed construction of a new state-of-the-art emergency suite that the city had awarded a Level I Trauma Center designation. This coveted assignment meant that the 911-system ambulances would bring all trauma cases within a certain catchment area. This would translate to nice increases in hospital revenue. The opening day ceremony went off with the usual fanfare, starting with an array of speeches by politicians, followed by the mayor's ribbon cutting. The CEO gave his usual recitation about human service and saving lives.

Soon thereafter, it became obvious that this new emergency department was defective in its design in that it was too small to meet the needs of the community. The area became so overcrowded that the management decided to "double-bunk" the patient cubicles. That meant putting two stretchers in a space the architects had designed for one. At times, the patients remained on the ambulance gurneys lined up in the corridor with the paramedics waiting more than an hour for an available emergency room bed. It was like watching the landed airplanes at LaGuardia Airport waiting on the tarmac for an open terminal. The walk-in patients had to wait ninety minutes just to see the triage nurse and nine hours for a doctor unless the nurse thought the patient might die in the waiting room. In those cases, the triage nurse would walk the patient into the main treatment area to be seated in a chair in front of the nurses' station. These poor souls usually waited two to three hours for a stretcher, and that was because the nurse considered them a high priority. One such patient, a seventy-three-year-old man, collapsed from his chair and had to be treated while lying on the floor for a few minutes because there was no place to put him until a stretcher appeared from the x-ray corridor (the patient in x-ray was probably wondering what happened to her stretcher).

This situation continued for about fourteen months, until there were so many complaints to the mayor's office that the mayor gave the CEO an ultimatum to fix the situation. The nursing director hired me to survey the emergency department and come up with some recommendations. I joined a committee of doctors, nurses, paramedics, and community leaders. We resolved most of the problems within two months. It was simply a matter of changing the mind-set of the professional staff, speeding up the process of making beds available on the floors, and decreasing the four-hour turnaround time for emergency room laboratory tests. We also stopped the practice of keeping admitted patients in the emergency department for diagnostic tests that doctors could perform in other areas and made a few other adjustments in handling the patient flow. The emergency department continued to have crowding problems, but it became tolerable. The point of this scenario is that these changes would not have taken place without community activism causing a barrage of complaints that triggered off a political backlash.

In brief, this story embodies the theory that the public's blind trust in the current corporate culture of hospital management is unjustifiable. How many people would be willing to fly if the airline industry reported 100,000 passenger deaths and 300,000 catastrophic injuries each year due to negligence or structural design defects? How long would you tolerate such performance?

The Liver Donor Tragedy

Another striking illustration of this point is the recently publicized case of a fifty-four-year-old man who allegedly died because of post-surgical negligence at a prestigious medical center in New York City. His wife charged that the people in control of the victim's postoperative care "showed a depraved indifference to human life." The New York State Health Department investigated the matter and cited the hospital for the postsurgical care, characterizing it as "inadequate and fragmented at best."

The man had been in good health when he went into the hospital to donate a portion of his liver to his younger brother. The next day he was dead. The wife related that her husband was exhibiting hiccups and nausea with increasing frequency and intensity. Then he vomited blood. There were a number of delayed responses from the nurses and one resident who allegedly did not seem concerned and did not appreciate the severity of the situation. Hiccups, nausea, and vomiting blood are classic signs of rupturing esophageal verices (varicose veins in the esophagus [food pipe]). There is increased pressure against the phrenic nerve, resulting in the uncontrollable hiccups. The usual cause is congestion in the portal vein (large vein drawing blood away from the liver). In any case, these symptoms were critical given that the surgeons had removed a portion of the patient's liver only a few hours earlier.

One remarkable aspect of this tragedy is the reported comment of the chief of staff. The *Newsday* reporter quoted him as having said, "We did what any ethical organization would do. We admitted that the postoperative care was not optimal in this case and we have fixed it. . . . This is a quality institution. . . . I don't believe we should be measured by a single case in a single point in time." The problem with this statement is that even a single case of neglect by a contingent of nurses and doctors being apathetic toward a series of life-threatening symptoms is exactly how one should measure the performance of a world-renowned hospital. It is highly unlikely that this apathy was an isolated incident that accidentally fell upon this poor fellow like a brick tumbling from a high-rise construction site. This endemic indifference and/or lack of basic knowledge was an indication of a deep-seated management infrastructure deficiency. The scariest part of the executive's quoted statement was "we have fixed it." This hospital manager seems to have missed the point in his zeal for protecting the reputation of a fine institution that pays him a six-figure salary. A young healthy man lost his life. He is gone forever. How does that get "fixed"? Moreover, this medical center had fifty-one malpractice cases pending against it on the New York State Supreme Court calendar as of May 30, 2002 (this does not include cases in discovery and those recently settled). Thus it was disingenuous to say that this was "a single case in a single point in time." This is an example of a hospital senior manager glossing over the real cause of the scandalous events in attempting to "fix" the institution's public image.

Despite that example, for the most part, hospital managers are well-educated, law-abiding, well-intentioned individuals. On the other hand, hospitals have evolved from a charitable institution type of structure relying heavily on donations to a cash-flow corporate culture relying almost exclusively on service revenues. Although profit motivation is not necessarily bad, the negative pressure of institutional budget deficits will send executives scrambling to cut costs and admit patients beyond total bed capacity. The overriding concern is that most hospitals experience cycles of cash-flow deficit because reimbursement does not keep up with overhead. This information, however, will only be useful if it teaches you how to differentiate a well-run hospital from one that should have a danger sign on the front door.

How to Find the Safest Hospital

For those of you who live in urban areas where there is more than one hospital to choose from, here is a list of what to look for when you engage in comparison "shopping." This is especially important if you move into a new area. You need to choose your hospital at least as carefully as you choose your schools and place of worship. They are not all the same.

Acceptable Hospital	Dangerous Hospital
Balanced budget	Cash-flow deficit
Good labor relations	Poor labor relations
All corridors clear	Equipment in corridors
Free of foul odors	Odor of human excrement coming from rooms
Care plan conferences include patient or family	Care plan conferences exclude patient or family
Operating room staffed twenty-four hours/day	Operating room closed at night with on-call staff
Nursing recruitment and retention program	No formal nursing recruitment and retention program
Staffing prescheduled with adequate numbers	Supervisors scramble desperately to find nurses
Zero tolerance for patient trauma	Some trauma seen as "unavoidable"
Patient satisfaction survey forms provided	No expression of interest in patient satisfaction

For those of you who live in less populated areas where there is only one hospital within a reasonable distance, you should make your inquiry to know your hospital's shortcomings so you can protect yourself and your family. In the succeeding chapters, you will learn how to do just that.

The Hospital's Finances

First, with regard to financial considerations, it is simple common sense. Some hospitals seem to have the money they need to carry out their day-to-day operations, while others are consistently broke. Whether that is the result of government cutbacks, poor planning, negligence, or outright theft, management cannot effectively run any organization that is chronically on the verge of bankruptcy. You can count on the management of such impoverished institutions to do something stupid and dangerous like justifying precariously low staffing levels for the sake of institutional survival. Thus the first item you should ask for when visiting your community hospital is a copy of the annual report. If the hospital does not publish one, it is usually required to file one with the state authorities. In most states, it is the department of health. You can log on to your state's website for details. Everyone who is going to use a hospital has a right to know its financial condition. Some of the better hospitals have websites that will tell you where to get a copy of their annual report. Another way to investigate your hospital's fiscal state of affairs is to check its credit rating. If you find that your hospital cannot pay its bills on time and has had to lay off its employees to reduce the payroll, find another facility. If the next one is too far away, proceed with caution and know that you can learn how to be in control of your safety (that's the purpose of this book).

Labor Relations at the Hospital

Second, concerning labor relations, this important factor can determine the quality of your care. Disgruntled employees are not the people I would want to rely on for safe health-care services. Moreover, hospital managers who deal with strikes by importing personnel to cross picket lines are wreaking havoc with life and limb. I have seen many help wanted ads for nurses from agencies who specialize in this endeavor. The large print says, "Nurses desperately needed for critical care, operating rooms and other areas, one hundred dollars per hour." The small print states, "Labor dispute exists." The hospital managers are not going to properly screen such nurses because this is not a normal hiring situation with multiple interviews and reference checks. Any nurse with a license and a warm body who is willing to cross a picket line and lacks professional ethics will be standing at your bedside. It does not take much for a physician or a nurse to inadvertently transform an intravenous medication to a lethal injection. If there is any history of a nurse's strike in your institution, call the Nurses' Association of your state and find out what the issues were and how the managers conducted themselves during the dispute. Again, if you cannot stay away from such a place, you should know the kind of people who are in command.

The State of the Corridors

Third, it is important to check the upper floor corridors for clutter. If you see unused beds and equipment lining the hallways, be aware that there is poor supervision from top to bottom. Seeing such muddle in areas that are supposed to be kept clear at all times should leave you wondering about equipment being in disrepair and not being fixed, infectious biohazard material lingering on objects that are not being cleaned, and where the supervisors are hiding. This deplorable situation when widely tolerated reflects wanton negligence on the part of the housekeeping, engineering, and nursing departments that are accountable for environmental cleanliness, safety, and patient well-being.

The Smell of the Place

Fourth, when you walk through your hospital, take a good whiff. If you smell feces or urine while moving through the hallway, chances are that someone is lying in it. It is also possible that an unfortunate soul had an accident on the floor and no one rushed to clean it up.

In either event, it takes some time for the odor to permeate the corridors. This is a telltale sign of reckless patient neglect. If you are already involved as a patient or visitor, the best way to deal with this appalling condition is to complain in the strongest possible terms to the CEO. If such a malodorous state exists, it is unlikely to be an isolated incident. The speed with which the administration responds is an indicator as to whether or not you should immediately look to transfer to another place, even if it is some distance away.

The Attitude of the Health-Care Team

Fifth, on the topic of team conferences, this is a meeting of various members of the health-care team usually comprising a physician, a nurse, a physical therapist, a social worker, a discharge planner, and representatives of other disciplines. These individuals come together to discuss the patient's condition and progress and to plan the next move. Over the past three decades, there has been a movement toward inviting the patient and/or family member to attend and participate in the planning. With the entire team arrayed before you, you have an excellent opportunity to ask any questions about the illness and possible complications and raise any concerns about safety and the quality of your services. The presence of such a program keeps all aspects of your care coordinated with you being the one in charge. Many medical centers have either done away with this practice or never implemented it. This is one of the first activities management eliminates as staffing numbers dwindle. Without such a team approach, the services are always fragmented, sometimes duplicated, and occasionally missing. You will see each of the members of the health-care "team" one by one without knowing if they ever talk to each other about your condition and treatment.

Operating Room Staffing

Sixth, about the subject of operating room staffing, this is a question of availability for people who need emergency surgery. It takes about thirty minutes to page the on-call personnel and wait for them to arrive. Additionally, it takes another thirty minutes to open an operating suite once it has been shut down for the night. If, heaven forbid, you had a ruptured appendix, a stab or gunshot wound, internal bleeding, or any other life-threatening emergency, would you want to wait an hour for the operating room to open for business? It is imperative to choose a hospital that has at least one circulating nurse, one scrub nurse, one anesthetist, and a complete array of surgical specialists in position to begin emergency surgery within a few minutes of the patient's arrival, twenty-four hours per day, seven days per week. If you cannot find such a facility in your community, you have a potential problem. One possible solution is to find out if the emergency medical service system has a helicopter on hand to evacuate critical individuals to a major medical center. Otherwise, you may have to engage in some community activism to improve the availability of surgical teams.

Nurse Recruitment and Retention

Seventh, pertaining to nursing employment, the adequacy of this workforce is the single most influential determinant of your safety and welfare or that of your loved one. Although Chapter 3 is entirely devoted to this crucial topic, I must include the general impact of nurse staffing as a vital part of the tool kit for your overall hospital evaluation. It is important to ask any one of the directors in the nursing office about the recruitment and retention program because there is a nationwide shortage in the human pool of hospital nurses. In some areas, the scarcity is critical. The statistics are easy to evaluate—compare the number of nurses who resigned over the last quarter with the number of new hires for general nursing and for each specialty. If the former is greater, you will need to know what the board of directors, CEO, and vice president of nursing services are doing about it. The most logical solution is to recruit from English-speaking foreign countries. If your hospital is not doing this, then the decision makers are obliged to explain what alternative measures are in place because if they are doing nothing, then the number of available nurses is shrinking. In that case, you can inevitably count on sharing one nurse with forty other patients. When you next visit the hospital (hopefully not as a patient), see how long it takes the nurse to answer a call for help. If your facility is not hiring at least as many nurses as are quitting every week, you can expect to triple the average response time in three or four months. Furthermore, the more the remaining nurses become overworked and exhausted, the more the attrition accelerates. As for the solution—nothing works better than a delegation of concerned citizens and a local politician demanding an answer from hospital administration as to what steps they are taking to resolve this dilemma.

Safe Staffing Levels

Eighth, included in the framework of safe staffing levels is the daily task of meeting the minimum requirements for any given shift. Actually, the primary responsibility falls on the staffing coordinators with regard to setting up schedules one month in advance. The final accountability for safe staffing levels falls on the nursing supervisor of the preceding shift. The prevailing practice as of this writing is for the coordinator to schedule employees and take no action to fill in the gaps, even if there is only one nurse scheduled for a seven-bed intensive care unit. The nursing supervisor then spends most of the shift scrambling for nurses, calling off-duty personnel and outside staffing agencies. You should go to the nursing office and ask, "What percentage of the minimum required number of nurses is on next month's staffing schedule?" In some cases, I have seen zero. If the number is chillingly low, you are not likely to receive a straight answer. So, why bother asking such a question? Because the more that people ask about staffing, the more nursing administrators will realize that there is public suspicion of how they are conducting their internal affairs. They are likely to respond accordingly and voluntarily improve their performance. Secrecy is the weapon by which bureaucrats defend the status quo and resist change. Questions are the daggers by which you can pierce the veil of concealment and transform the reticent bureaucracy to a responsive administration.

Patient Trauma

Ninth, there is the enigma of patient trauma being "unavoidable." From a legal perspective, the occurrence of an injurious traumatic event does not, by itself, prove negligence. If the admitting nurse, in making an assessment by current standards, did not consider the patient to have been at risk of falling and there was no compelling reason for the nurse to be at the bedside at the time of the accident, then there cannot be a finding of negligence. In short, the generally accepted standards of nursing practice do not require the hospital staff to observe all patients at all times. Such standards only require nurses to take reasonable precautions. Hence, the question is, "What is missing in the fall prevention protocol that has so many people plummeting unpredictably to the floor?" The answer is surveillance. The more surveillance there is, the less people will fall—simple logic. Consequently, the attitude of senior-level officials is of paramount importance. When you ask the obvious question "What assurance can you give me that my [mother, father, wife, husband, child, etc.] won't fall and get hurt?" the answer you need to look for is "Let's talk about things we can do together to prevent such a terrible thing from happening." If you do not get the opportunity for such dialogue, take control of safety and prevention by remaining at the bedside. You will then have to rely on your own judgment as to whether you can leave and for how long. You might elicit the help of other family members to take turns.

Patient Satisfaction Surveys

Tenth, there is a new catchphrase in hospital management chat—"customer service." The thought was for staff members to develop the attitude that patients ought to be regarded as customers who could take their patronage elsewhere if not satisfied. This business-oriented approach is actually a positive aspect because it causes employees to work toward making the hospital stay a satisfying experience. If you cannot find a satisfaction survey form, then try to find another hospital or write a letter detailing what you like and dislike about the facility and its services and hand deliver it to the executive officers.

You as Team Leader

In summary, all acute care hospitals in the United States operate under a uniform set of standards promulgated by the Joint Commission on Accreditation of Healthcare Organizations (JCAHO). This private regulatory agency surveys all member institutions once every three years to see if they are meeting standards, including various protocols encompassing safety, comfort, education, and skill levels of caregivers. The surveyors review every aspect of hospital management—for example, medicine, nursing, therapies, housekeeping, infection control, building maintenance engineering, and biomedical engineering. This process, briefly, is a major component of the "health-care system." The sad fact is that with 100,000 deaths and approximately 300,000 catastrophic injuries every year, the system is an abject failure in the context of providing safety, comfort, and dignity to its patrons. In order to understand why, we need to ask the question, "What's missing?" One answer is your participation.

Consequently, you must take your rightful position as the leader of your health-care team for either yourself or someone for whom you are making all health-related decisions. As team leader, you are in command. The tools you will need to make good decisions regarding safety, comfort, and dignity are contained in this book. We have started with the information required to tell whether a hospital is reasonably safe or downright dangerous.

Scoring Hospital Safety

Here is a consumer's checklist to score your hospital's safety on a scale of 1 to 10. Remember that even if your hospital scores 10, you will need to take some measures to protect yourself or your loved ones.

Hospital Checklist	Score (1 for yes, 0 for no)
Balanced budget	
Good labor relations	
All corridors clear	
Free of foul odors	
Care plan conferences include patient or family	
Operating room staffed twenty-four hours/day	
Nursing recruitment and retention program	
Staffing prescheduled with adequate numbers	
Zero tolerance for patient trauma	
Patient satisfaction survey forms provided	
Total score	

2

The Emergency Waiting Game

THE EMERGENCY ROOM is the place where most of us enter the health-care system. Many are there with undiagnosed life-threatening conditions when they first arrive. Their survival depends on how fast and accurately the staffers diagnose and treat their problems. Most emergency rooms can at times get so crammed full that they become unsafe. Even an anthill will implode if you put too many ants in it. Accordingly, there are three determining factors in getting—or preventing—a good result in the emergency department. These are triage, waiting time, and capacity. First, the overlying problem is that at most times in any emergency room there is only one physician for dozens of people. The nurse-to-patient ratio is usually about fifty to one, counting those in the waiting room. Thus it is not possible to take care of everyone without making people wait for several hours. That is why one of the registered nurses must provide triage services. Triage is a nursing assessment made to determine the level of urgency of the patients' need for medical intervention—who can wait and who is likely to die in the waiting room.

How Triage Works

Emergency departments are places that have waves of people coming in by ambulance, by private car, on foot, and, in some cases, by helicopter. These people have all kinds of problems with all levels of severity. The nurses and doctors often endure unreasonable amounts of stress and suffer from exhaustion as there are usually more patients than they can safely handle at any one time. As long as this continues, there will be casualties in terms of people dying with treatable conditions.

A Fatal Triage Error

A case in point is the premature death of a thirty-eight-year-old mother of three. One Friday morning during the summer of 2000, Mrs. K. was traveling with her husband via the subway on their usual commute to their respective jobs in Manhattan when she fell and hit the back of her head against a pole as the train jerked forward. She grappled with the intense pain for a moment and then regained her composure. Mr. K. asked his wife, "Are you all right? Do you want me to bring you to the hospital?"

"No, I'll be okay. Just walk me to my job." Mr. K. accompanied her to the bank where she worked as a loan officer. Mrs. K. spent most of the day fighting headache and dizziness, unable to focus on her work. After she told her boss what had happened, he advised her to go home around 3 P.M. She called her husband and he brought her to their home in Queens. The rest of the weekend, Mrs. K. stayed in bed with a slight headache, but she was able to sleep after taking Tylenol.

When Monday came, Mrs. K. went to work again. She was still dizzy and unable to focus on her job. She called her husband again, and he took her to the emergency room in one of the several world-famous New York City medical centers.

When they arrived at the hospital, the waiting room was mostly full, with only a few vacant seats. They went into a small cubicle on the side to see the triage nurse. The nurse wrote in the triage notes,

"Complains of headache since Friday. She claims she hit her head on subway." The nurse then took Mrs. K.'s vital signs (measurement of temperature, pulse rate, respiratory rate, blood pressure, and oxygen saturation). The readings were all within normal limits, and the nurse observed that Mrs. K. walked in with a steady gait. Thinking that the patient should have gone to her private physician instead of wasting the emergency department resources, the nurse assigned the lowest priority level and told Mr. K. to take his wife to the walk-in clinic down the hall, saying, "There's going to be a four-hour wait. They are crowded and we are short of help today."

When Mrs. K. tried to get up, her legs buckled. She was still conscious but was unable to get out of the chair. The nurse, convinced that her initial assessment was correct, believed that Mrs. K. was putting on a dramatic performance in order to get faster service. Therefore, she reluctantly offered a stretcher and helped Mrs. K. to climb on to it with the husband supporting her other arm.

Then the nurse rolled the stretcher out into the hallway and went back to her desk. She called the charge nurse in the main emergency treatment area to report the case and said, "I've got a drama queen here who claimed that she is too weak to stand up after I told her she would have to go to walk-in and wait a few hours for a doctor. Her vitals are fine. She walked in with her husband and said she has a headache after allegedly hitting her head in the subway three days ago. Where do you want her?"

"Did you put her on a stretcher?"

"Yes, what else could I do?"

"I have no space in here. It is a zoo. Where is she?"

"I put her in corridor A, and I sent the husband to registration."

"Okay, we'll come and get her as soon as we have an opening, if no real emergencies show up between now and then. She'll probably end up waiting longer than she would in walk-in."

About thirty minutes later, Mr. K. came back from registration and could not find his wife. He had to wait five minutes for the triage nurse to finish with another patient before she would show him where to find corridor A. When he went up to his wife, she was lying on her back and not moving. He nudged her shoulders, and she opened her eyes and spoke with slurred speech, looking confused. He went back to triage and found the nurse with yet another patient. He blurted out, "There is something wrong with my wife! She is difficult to arouse and she has slurred speech!"

The nurse replied, "I'll take a look at her in a few minutes."

"But my wife needs help now!"

"Your wife is fine. I will be there in a short while. I have nine people waiting to be triaged. As soon as I have finished, I'll come and look."

Mr. K. threw up his hands in frustration and went back to his wife. She was still arousable but stuporous. He waited another twenty minutes and no one came. He went back to the triage nurse and told her he was very concerned and demanded immediate medical attention. The nurse gave him the same reply as if it were prerecorded. This back-and-forth continued every ten minutes for another hour until Mr. K. found a different nurse and asked, "What happened to the other woman?"

"She went on her dinner break," was the reply.

"Please come and look at my wife. I am having a hard time keeping her awake, and she has been in the hallway on a stretcher for almost two hours. Please!"

The relief nurse became alarmed at what she heard. She immediately went over to Mrs. K. and found her completely unresponsive. She sounded the alarm, and suddenly an array of doctors, nurses, and medical students appeared and rolled Mrs. K. into one of the code rooms (space designed for life support). Within a few minutes, Mrs. K. had an intravenous line and an endotracheal (breathing) tube. A transporter brought her to radiology, where a CAT (computerized axial tomography) scan revealed a large hematoma (blood clot) on the brain. Apparently, the head trauma on the subway train three days earlier had caused a slow hemorrhage in the back of her head that ultimately produced continuously increasing pressure within the skull. In less than thirty minutes, Mrs. K. was in the operating room undergoing neurosurgery for removal of the clot and cauterization of the bleeding vessels. She remained in a coma for eight months and died without ever regaining consciousness. Too much time had passed, causing irreversible brain damage.

In this case, there was no problem with the skill and efficiency of the emergency department staff in general. The quandary was one triage nurse with a bad attitude. When Mr. K. left his wife to take care of her paperwork, he, in effect, put the life of the mother of his children in that nurse's hands. When she said, "As soon as I have finished, I'll come and look," Mr. K. had to believe that once his wife was on a stretcher, she would get prompt medical attention. If he had not had that typical mistaken confidence in the health-care system, he might have been alarmed at the nurse's initial low-priority assignment, refused to leave his wife's presence, and vociferously demanded immediate medical attention from hospital management.

Triage Priority Levels

The general standard for emergency departments is to have five levels of priority: code, critical, urgent, nonurgent disabled, and ambulatory.

Code. The code level refers to someone who has suffered cardiac arrest outside of the hospital or someone whose vital signs crash within the emergency department. Resuscitation efforts are in progress. These cases do not go to triage. They go straight into the code or trauma room, where, usually, there is a team standing by. This category also includes people with gunshot or stab wounds with possible vital organ involvement and/or altered or absent vital signs.

Critical. The critical designation denotes a person with stable vital signs who is exhibiting symptoms or who gives a history that clearly delineates a life-threatening condition. This might be a patient with chest pain, shortness of breath, and profuse sweating (diaphoresis). This also would include people who have a history of vomiting blood, multiple traumas with head injury, or a gunshot or stab wound, as well as asthmatics, diabetics with low blood sugar or extremely high blood sugar, and the like. The triage nurse usually sees these people first and should hand them over immediately to the doctors. In some cases, the nurse can administer initial treatment under standing orders, such as oxygen or a dextrose (simple sugar) injection for the diabetic who is crashing from low blood sugar (hypoglycemia). No time should be wasted in treating these individuals.

Urgent. The urgent category, as usually described in hospital manuals, represents patients with serious conditions requiring medical intervention within two hours. More specifically, a doctor should see patients with an urgent need within one hour; these patients should never wait more than two hours. These are people with abdominal pain, high fever and/or productive cough, deep lacerations with bleeding under control, closed fractures with deformity, and so on. If the emergency department is so overwhelmed that the triage nurse can anticipate a longer wait, he or she has an obligation to monitor such a patient for changes in symptoms with vital sign measurement at least once every hour. Accepted standards of care also require that these persons be lying on a stretcher and not sitting in a chair.

Nonurgent disabled. The nonurgent disabled individuals, unable to walk or remain in a chair, are those for whom the triage nurse determines that up to a four-hour wait is clinically acceptable. The acceptable standards require that the triage nurse place these people on a stretcher for comfort and safety. Sometimes the disability relates to the presenting problem, such as a herniated disc causing severe low back pain. With others, the disability does not seem related, as with nursing home residents who arrive because their feeding stomach tube or bladder urine-draining tube has become dislodged. This creates a problem because most of those transferees do not need to be in an emergency room. A physician could easily replace the tubes at the nursing home.

Notwithstanding the practical considerations, the health-care reimbursement system provides nursing home operators with financial incentives for transferring their residents to occupy space in the hospital emergency department. This is especially incomprehensible since it would be a great deal less traumatic to the frail elderly to remain in their quiet, peaceful, familiar beds rather than having strangers uproot them to the noisy, overcrowded emergency room. Nonetheless, the government would rather waste an extra three thousand tax dollars for the ambulance and hospital charges and prevent patients with real crises from having access to the emergency room bed. This is a defect in the health-care bureaucracy that indirectly kills people and causes the elderly to suffer mental anguish.

Ambulatory. Lastly, the ambulatory patients are those who do not need emergency care but are there anyway with colds, toothaches, headaches, bumps, bruises, abrasions, small lacerations, skin rashes, and so on. This usually makes up the majority of the waiting room population. This is why emergency departments need triage. The more progressive hospitals have a twenty-four hour walk-in clinic to relieve the burden of the emergency areas. However, the principle standard of any triage nurse is to err on the side of caution. Thus many people who would do well with the clinic will remain in the emergency department.

To conclude with regard to triage, it is important to ask the triage nurse, "What level of priority did you assign?" Then ask for the rationale. If he or she sends you to the walk-in clinic with abdominal pain, nausea, diarrhea, fever, and/or a severe headache following head trauma, you have a problem. You are supposed to be on a stretcher with an intravenous line and with a blood specimen drawn, tagged, and bagged for the laboratory. The triage nurse need not have the last word. You have a right to ask for the charge nurse or supervisor to reassess the situation and countermand the initial decision.

Emergency Room Waiting Time

There is a relationship between how long patients have to wait to see a physician and the outcome. Injuries and illnesses that need medical and nursing intervention are time sensitive. The longer the wait, the more damage occurs because there is a loss and/or deprivation of basic needs for survival, such as oxygen, blood, electrolytes (potassium, sodium, etc.), sugar, water, immunity, skin integrity, and the like. Additionally, waiting time in the emergency department is determined, in part, by factors such as the ratio of physician and nurse to patient, laboratory turnaround time, x-ray turnaround time, and average length of stay.

These factors are obviously interdependent. Most urban emergency rooms are overwhelmed and overcrowded. For some it is occasional, but for most it is the norm. Health-care planners do not seem to be assessing community needs before pouring the cement. The planners are building the emergency rooms too small, and the number of doctors and nurses are too few to provide safe care for the overwhelming numbers that converge at the door. This is a bizarre phenomenon because it defies logic. It would seem that the faster they move the patients through the system, the more revenue there will be.

Upon closer examination, you would find some correctable contributing factors, such as waiting four hours for the results of a ten-minute laboratory test, inadequate staffing of nurses and technicians, and/or lack of prompt response from on-call specialists.

Additionally, patients who have completed the diagnosis and stabilization process remain in the treatment area waiting for a bed or for transportation. Thus if a patient hangs around for two hours for the ambulance to bring him or her back to the nursing home, the next person then has to wait two hours for that space to become available.

Moreover, when such conditions exist with hundreds of people moving around in a frenzy, the state of affairs usually becomes chaotic and confusing. Charts are misplaced, specimens do not get to the laboratory, the doctors cannot find the x-rays, and sometimes the nurses have to go look for their patients. These situations further slow the process. Accordingly, the people who manage the emergency rooms need to develop a new model of patient-flow dynamics because the current design is simply not working.

What's more, on the subject of overcrowding in the emergency department, the lack of available beds in the respective intensive care units and/or floor exacerbates the overloading. Hospital managers in many instances are loath to divert incoming patients to other facilities because it translates to a loss of revenue. Frequently, under such management, doctors admit patients and hold them in the emergency department until a bed opens up, which could take days. This deplorable policy has been common practice for the entire twenty-seven years that I have been a nurse, and it continues to this day. I have experienced this predicament as both a nurse and a patient. I once stayed at Montefiore Medical Center in 1986 on an emergency room stretcher for two days. It was pure torture. The stretcher was too narrow and too hard. I was lying on a metal platform with a thin foam rubber slab between it and my backside. The resultant pressure was painful. The reason given for this torment was that there were no beds available. The management should have offered me an opportunity to transfer to another hospital in the area, but that was not an available option because the system was not set up for true customer service. Considerations like safety, comfort, and dignity are not a part of the policy-making process.

Finally, the emergency room is not equipped to house patients for more than four hours at a time. If waiting for a bed causes the patient to remain longer than that, the quality of care falls below standard. The emergency room nurses cannot reasonably provide for the needs of new arrivals and give the time and attention required for a proper nursing assessment and management of the admitted patient's condition.

The solution to the universal emergency department debacle is complex. Certainly, if you have been waiting several hours, you would feel restless, frustrated, and angry. You might even worry that something bad will happen if you do not get to see a doctor in the next few seconds. The situation can get very ugly at this point. Once, an emergency department administrator got an inspiration to bring in a magic show to entertain the people in the waiting room and ease the tension. It had the opposite effect, and the magician had to disappear. Although he was good at his craft, he was playing to the wrong audience. One man told him where to shove his rabbit, and a woman shouted, "Why don't you conjure me up a doctor so that I can get treated for this lousy migraine!" When the performer pulled out his rope trick, another man told him to go hang himself with the rope.

But it is important to know that loud complaints are counter-productive. The last thing you need is to cause the nurses and doctors to want to avoid you. Once it becomes apparent that you have waited too long, you need to understand that the triage nurse has decided that the patients going ahead of you would have a higher risk than you of dying without prompt attention. This does not mean you have no risk. This is a comparison of your risk against that of others, and you came out on the bottom. Remember that the triage nurse is simply choosing between two or more people to fill one vacant slot.

While being careful not to displace another person who would need medical attention sooner than you might, you can take a few actions that might reduce your waiting time:

- Ask the triage nurse to give the rationale for your low priority.
- If you feel your symptoms have gotten worse, report it and say that you feel your condition is deteriorating.
- If you believe that the decision to make you wait is not correct, call the nursing supervisor.
- Remain truthful about your symptoms and don't exaggerate.
- Do not lie on the floor pretending to have passed out. You will not likely be able to fool the nurses and doctors, and if you do, you could get the wrong treatment.

Once you are inside you will likely experience more waiting for blood and urine tests and/or x-rays. This will take another four to six hours. The best way to approach this is to let the charge nurse or supervisor know that you are aware that a lab test takes no more than a few minutes and that an x-ray takes ninety seconds. At this point, you can ask a staff member to call the laboratory or x-ray department to find out what is going on. However, it is important to realize that this situation is not going to improve instantaneously. The most common reason for such delays is simply that the laboratory and x-ray facilities and the personnel are inadequate in meeting demand. Increasing such resources would require an act from top-level executives committed to improving emergency services.

Furthermore, the hospital administrators have the option of going on diversion. This is simply calling the 911 dispatch office to report that the hospital is over capacity and that ambulances need to divert patients to alternative facilities. There are capacity ordinances in every municipality governing all public places, like theaters, restaurants, and houses of worship. Why do the local governments allow hospital executives to cram in more people than they can safely handle? In this situation it is not a matter of being unsafe in case of fire—it is unsafe as it is. Thus if you find yourself sitting in the emergency waiting room for several hours and the place is jam-packed with people, ask the nursing supervisor if the emergency room has been placed on diversion. If it has not, then ask, "Why not?" I do not know what answer you will get, but it is the question that matters. The question, if repeated often enough by many different people, will make decision makers realize that the public is mistrustful of their management policies.

To offer some additional solutions, there are some emergency centers that are managed better than others. It is important to be able to choose one that will give you and your family a better chance for the most effective care possible should you ever need it. You will need to make such a choice as soon as possible, because you would not have time to make a selection during an emergency. You should know where each emergency room is located in your area and the shortest route to get there. It would also be advisable to make an appointment with the emergency department administrator to inquire about the quality of care in his or her emergency room. Here is a list of questions to ask:

- How many attending doctors are on duty at any one time and is that number consistent with established policy?
- How many nurses are on duty during each shift and how many are supposed to be on duty?

- How many patients can you fit in the treatment areas at any one time?
- Are the attending physicians board certified in emergency medicine?
- Do your nurses and doctors have the certification to provide advanced adult and pediatric life support?
- Do you have a trauma team?
- May I see your list of specialists on call?
- If I need a specialist that is not on your list, where will you transfer me and how long will that take?
- What is your policy on leaving patients in other areas such as the x-ray department?

To begin with, getting answers to the first three questions will enable you to calculate how many people each doctor and nurse can take care of at any moment in time. If the ratio is greater than ten patients for every one doctor or five patients for every one nurse, that emergency department is understaffed and unsafe. You should tell the administrator that this is unacceptable. Expressing your concern and encouraging others to do the same begins a process of cumulative feedback that will ultimately have a positive effect.

Secondly, aside from making sure that the staff members have the right credentials, the issue of available specialists is a crucial matter. Not every hospital has the ability to handle critical emergencies such as brain hemorrhage or stab and gunshot wounds. You should find out what specialties are available and the usual response time once the emergency attending makes the call. I once triaged a twenty-five-year-old woman who came in looking extremely pale with low blood pressure and abdominal pain. I treated her for shock and called in a request for immediate attention. The emergency attending physician came out, made a fast assessment, and decided that we were dealing with an ectopic pregnancy (the embryo attached itself inside the fallopian tube), which is life-threatening. She called the gynecologist, who got there in five minutes, and the patient was in the operating room within thirty minutes of her arrival and ultimately recovered. In this case, the successful outcome was almost entirely dependent on the prompt response of the specialist.

Finally, one of the most common mistakes made in emergency nursing care is leaving patients in areas outside of the emergency department. This happens most frequently in the x-ray department corridor. The patient is either waiting for the x-ray technician or waiting to be brought back to the emergency room. Too often such people experience a potentially life-threatening crisis with no one in attendance, such as a semiconscious sixty-eight-year-old woman who vomited and choked while lying supine on an emergency room stretcher. The nurse decided to leave the patient alone for a few minutes to avoid exposure to the x-rays. Within the time it took to shoot an abdominal film, the woman's stomach contents went into her lungs. The result was extensive brain damage and death two days later. If the nurse had donned a lead apron and remained with the patient while the x-rays were being taken, she could have turned the woman's head to one side and prevented the choking. Thus since such occurrences are unpredictable, there should be a nurse in attendance at all times with patients who have an altered level of consciousness.

In summary, the emergency department is a place to which many people owe their lives. When properly run, it is the only safe haven for many hurting and frightened folks. Unfortunately, if you have ever been to one, you know that virtually every emergency room in existence is too small and has too few nurses and doctors to provide timely treatment to all who turn up. It usually looks like there has been a disaster causing massive casualties. There seems to be a universal belief among those who plan and manage that an overcrowded emergency room serves the financial needs of the institution. Otherwise, the spaces would be larger, there would be more staff, and, unless there is a real calamity, waiting time of more than one hour would be astonishing.

As you make your rounds to evaluate the safety of the emergency departments in your area, use the following comparative tool.

INSIDER TIPS

Comparing a Safe Emergency Room with a Dangerous One

Reasonably Safe Emergency Department	Dangerous Emergency Department
Average doctor-to-patient ratio of one to ten	Average doctor-to-patient ratio of one to more than ten
Average nurse-to-patient ratio of one to five	Average nurse-to-patient ratio of one to more than five
Keeps statistics on waiting time and has as goal to average one hour or less	Does not follow waiting time and/or has no formal program to reduce it
Allows nursing supervisor to call for ambulance diversion when filled to capacity	Has unwritten policy against going on diversion to avoid losing revenue
Maintains strict policy on assigning only nurses with proper credentials and orientation	Uses temp-agency nurses without adequate orientation
Has a written protocol for stabilizing and transferring patients with problems requiring treatment at another hospital	No such protocol in place or not reviewed and updated every three months
Keeps a list of on-call specialists and contacts each daily to confirm availability and response time	No calls made to specialists each day to confirm availability
Has strict policy on keeping patients under close observation until medically cleared	No such policy in place
Does not keep new admissions in emergency department for more than four hours; transfers admitted patients without beds to other hospitals	Will keep admitted patients indefinitely in the emergency department until bed opens up; transfers admitted patients only upon demand

3

Staying Safe on a Hospital Floor

CERTAIN ERRORS THAT can endanger patients are relatively common in the management of a medical or surgical hospital floor. The key to avoiding many of these dangers is never to assume that the hospital management is operating the floor the way it should. That would be like buying a used car and driving it at high speeds without first testing the brakes. Find out how well the administrators are managing the area by making some basic inquiries. The most important questions that you (as the patient or concerned family member or friend) need to pose when arriving for the first time on a typical hospital floor are as follows:

- How far away is the patient from the nurses' station?
- Does the floor have all the necessary equipment and supplies and are the machines in good working order?
- Who is in charge of the nursing care?
- Who is in charge of the nurses?
- What is the nurse-to-patient ratio (how many patients does each nurse have to take care of)?

- What is the patient acuity on this floor (how sick are the other patients by comparison)?
- Who is the attending physician and how involved will he or she be in the patient's case?
- Who is actually going to write the patient's orders?
- Who are the specialists on call?

Distance to the Nurses

The question of distance is almost self-explanatory. Whenever I see a hospital floor that has the nurses' station at one end of a long corridor, it is obvious that the architect did not get input from nurses in creating such a design. The farther away a patient is from the nurses' station, the less attention the patient will get. Someone should have asked the planners, "If you or someone you love is in the hospital, how far would you want the nurse to walk to get to you in case of an emergency?" One might also have asked, "If you had to scream for help, would you want no one to be able to hear you?"

The prudent charge nurse will assess how much attention you will need in deciding whether you should be placed nearby or far off. If the floor is full and everyone needs frequent observation (high acuity), there is a problem. About a third of the patients will be lacking some measure of prompt attention to their needs. I have reviewed dozens of cases over the last eighteen years in which a staff member found the patient dead and no one could tell when the poor soul stopped breathing. These unfortunates were always more than five doors away from the nurses' station.

However, even though tearing down and rebuilding is often not feasible, a viable solution to this problem exists. There is no reason why the nurses have to all sit in one central area. With a moderate amount of interior remodeling, the hospital carpenters and maintenance workers can reduce the large central office area and create substations so that no bed is more than five doors away from a nurse's desk. Every patient should be within earshot of a nurse or an ancillary staff member at all times. Any hospital executive who says that is impossible is accepting occasional patient neglect as "unfortunate but unavoidable."

One occurrence that illustrates the perils of housing patients at an unsafe distance from the nurses' station is the case of the nineteen-year-old woman who hanged herself using the privacy curtain in a room of one of the city hospitals in New York a few years ago. She was a psychiatric patient hospitalized for severe depression. The psychiatrist cleared her for transfer to a regular hospital room because of a kidney infection. The young woman's need for intravenous antibiotics made the medical-surgical floor more expedient. She was in a semiprivate room that was too far away for anyone to hear her roommate yelling for help—the result being that the nurses were too late to save her. Even if the roommate had thought of using the call button in the middle of watching someone hanging herself by the neck, the room was too far away for a timely response.

Another case in point related to distance is a fifty-three-year-old man who stopped breathing after the nurses overmedicated him with morphine and sleeping pills. He had been complaining of severe pain after abdominal surgery. His wife discovered his body during visiting hours approximately two hours after he died. He was at the end of the corridor away from the nurses' station, and no one made rounds to check his condition for that period. Although there was the issue of being overmedicated followed by wanton neglect, this scenario exemplifies that being out of sight and out of earshot increases the likelihood of a less-than-diligent staff forgetting and neglecting the patients.

Life-Support Equipment

Moving to the issue of life-support equipment, supplies, and qualified personnel, having those available in case of emergency is vital indeed. When you arrive on a hospital floor as either a patient or family member, do you think about whether all the paraphernalia needed for lifesaving measures is immediately available? If you are like most consumers, that would be the furthest thing from your mind. After all, who are we to tell the health-care professionals how to do their jobs? Although for the most part there are systems in place to check the supplies and equipment at the beginning of every shift, people sometimes fail to perform routine rudimentary tasks. Sometimes the nurses report a broken or missing piece of equipment to management and nothing happens. The other problem is that usually there is only enough emergency equipment to manage two simultaneous crises on any one floor. Thus if a third emergency arises, the nurses have to waste time borrowing from another floor or ordering from the pharmacy or central supply.

The following is a list of items needed on every floor, which should be contained within a standard crash cart:

defibrillator
cardiac rhythm monitor (sometimes built into defibrillator)
intubation tray
tracheotomy tray
endotracheal tubes of all standard sizes
emergency drugs such as sodium bicarbonate, atropine,
    epinephrine (adrenalin), diuretics, antihistamines,
    antiarrhythmics, antihypertensives, insulin, and others
bladder catheters with drainage bags
syringes of all standard sizes
needles of all standard sizes
sterile kits containing gloves, tourniquets, gauze pads,
    disinfectant solution, antibacterial ointment, and tape
intravenous catheters of all standard sizes
intravenous solutions of all standard types
blood specimen containers for laboratory tests

You should never stay on a floor without receiving assurances that someone checked the crash cart to make sure that it has all required items in good working order.

A case to illustrate this point is an incident involving seventy-three-year-old "Sadie." She was seriously ill, but she might have had more time in relationship with her forty-seven-year-old daughter, "Norma," if not for the shameful fiasco that occurred during the attempt to save her life. Sadie entered the hospital with congestive heart failure. The heart loses its effectiveness as a pump in that condition. Moreover, fluid begins to back up, causing swelling inside the lungs and elsewhere in the body. Sadie's doctor admitted her because she was having some difficulty breathing, and he felt that a thorough workup and medical management would likely help her to avert a catastrophe. The reasoning was that if she were to encounter a crisis during this period, being in a hospital would assure her of having qualified personnel with lifesaving drugs and equipment at the ready. Little did the physician suspect that his patient would have been better off staying home with her daughter and relying on the paramedics responding to a 911 call.

Soon after she settled in, with her daughter at her bedside, Sadie gasped for air and collapsed in bed. Norma called out for help (she was near the nurses' station), and within seconds, there were four doctors and three nurses at the bedside with the crash cart. The cardiac monitor showed a straight line. Two members of the team started cardiopulmonary resuscitation (CPR), one providing respiration with a mask and ambu-bag (manually operated air pump) while the other administered chest compressions. Then the doctor in charge ordered sodium bicarbonate, epinephrine, and atropine. Up to this point, everything was well coordinated, and each member of the team knew exactly what his or her job was. What happened thereafter was a series of delays due to missing supplies and faulty equipment.

A few minutes into the code, the on-call anesthesiology resident showed up to intubate (pass a tube into the windpipe). This was the only way to assure that the air pumped in would go into the lungs and not the stomach. The anesthesiologist called for a certain size tube. There was none on the crash cart. One of the nurses had to run down the hall about forty or fifty feet to the other crash cart and run back with the tube. This was a loss of three minutes. While the nurse was running, the ordering doctor decided to defibrillate in an attempt to convert the heart to normal rhythm. One of the other doctors applied the paddles and fired—nothing happened. One of the other nurses hit the recharge button, and the familiar high-pitched squeal sounded off indicating the recharge was taking place. The doctor applied the paddles—and again nothing happened.

By this time, the first nurse had returned with the tube but then had to run back again to get the other defibrillator. This was another three-minute loss. In the interim, the nursing supervisor had arrived and immediately went to the adjacent floor and rolled in another crash cart as a backup. The second defibrillator did not work either until the supervisor pointed out that someone had disconnected the paddle unit. One quick "click" and the paddles fired off the power needed for the conversion. The heartbeat returned, but the rhythm deteriorated to a lethally slow rate of twenty beats per minute. The doctor ordered another bolus of atropine, but there was none on the cart. The supervisor produced one from the extra cart that she had brought with her.

The code proceeded for another thirty minutes, with the charge physician saying early on, "This woman is too far gone for us to do anything for her. Technically, she is already dead. We're just going through the motions for the benefit of the daughter, who is at the other side of that door."

Meanwhile, Norma was pacing in the corridor just outside the room, thinking all the while that her mom was getting the best possible care. Finally, the supervisor approached Norma at the doctor's behest, saying, "Your mother is gone. We did everything we could, and we were unable to save her." Norma's emotions changed from worry to disbelief and then to grief.

Retrospectively, it is impossible to know whether Sadie could have lived if the necessary items had been available when needed. Nonetheless, the loss of those costly moments forever robbed her of whatever prospect she had for survival. Ironically, Norma, being ignorant of the procedural chaos, accepted that it was her mother's time to die. It may have been her time, but the final botched attempt to save Sadie's life has to be characterized as sloppy.

The fact is that the potential for disaster in every hospital is an ever-present reality. When you first arrive as a patient or family member, it is vital to speak to the charge nurse and ask to see where the crash cart is located. Find out if the nurses are checking the equipment and supplies at the beginning of every shift. Ask the nurse to explain how long it will take the code team to respond when called. Finally, find out if any of the nurses on the floor have achieved certification in advanced cardiac life support (ACLS). Such questions would serve as a reminder to those who need it. If the answers leave you feeling unsafe, speak to the director of nursing and lodge a protest.

By comparison, whenever we board a commercial airliner or say good-bye to a loved one at the airport, we have confidence that the pilot and crew members will check all of their equipment and review emergency procedures before each flight. In this case, however, their lives are on the line the same as the passengers, so, to some degree, self-preservation motivates perfectionism. If all hospital personnel were like-minded at the start of each shift, there would almost certainly be much fewer adverse incidents related to faulty equipment, missing supplies, and/or bungled procedures.

Know Who Is Handling Nursing Care

Turning to the matter of the bedside registered nurse, the credentials, experience, and approach of this individual are central to the issues of quality and safety. In most cases, your nurse will conduct an intake interview as part of the admission process. Just as your nurse is assessing you as a patient, you should be assessing the nurse. Some of the information you need you can glean from the initial interview, because your nurse is required to give you a complete explanation of the hospital routine. Subsequently, the nurse will usually end with asking, "Do you have any questions?" This is your opportunity to turn the nurse-patient relationship into a team effort and take control of your well-being by making the following queries:

- How long have you been a nurse?
- How many times before have you performed the procedures that the doctor ordered?
- Can you explain what each of my medications is for and what possible side effects we have to watch out for?
- What would you do if one of the residents or interns writes an order that you think is contraindicated or might not be in my best interest?

- What precautions should we take to make certain that I don't fall and hurt myself?
- What precautions should we take to make certain that I don't get any bedsores?

An Experienced Nurse

First, it is in the standard patient's bill of rights that you are entitled to competent care provided by qualified personnel. Registered nurses in charge of your needs have a certain amount of autonomy in exercising clinical judgment to the extent that they are supposed to observe for any changes in your condition and report those to your attending physician or the physician's designee (usually a resident, house physician, physician assistant, or nurse practitioner). Therefore, you have a right to expect the nurse to have a certain amount of experience. A minimum of one year would be reasonable. A nurse with less time on the job would also be acceptable as long as there is a buddy system that pairs off the neophyte with a seasoned veteran.

A Skilled Nurse

Registered nurses are licensed to start intravenous lines, give injections, insert nasogastric tubes (through the nose and into the stomach), change sterile dressings, pack wound cavities, perform digital disimpaction, provide enemas, and insert urinary catheters into the bladder, just to name a few. The hospital management must allow you to have a reasonable level of comfort that the nurses are competent in performing whatever measures you need. Every hospital job application must include a skill checklist that documents the amount of experience a nurse has in performing all procedures. Additionally, a nursing education department is responsible for monitoring the skill level of all staff and per diem nurses. Thus you as the patient or family member should be entitled to such information as pertains to the services provided.

A case in point regarding the importance of assessing nursing skills is that of a man I'll call John Millhouse, who in August of 1995 entered a well-known cardiac surgery specialty hospital for a valve replacement. The surgery was successful. The problem started when John's blood test came in positive for tertiary syphilis. John had contracted syphilis during his days as a young Marine while on liberty in Seoul during the Korean War and had received penicillin for treatment. He did not quite get rid of the bug, so it flared up ten years later in chronic stage, and the doctor repeated the treatment in larger doses and over a longer period. The blood test at "Cardiac Hospital" only showed a prior exposure. Nonetheless, the infectious disease consultant wanted to treat John prophylactically with an intramuscular penicillin injection. The cardiac surgeon concurred and wrote the order.

A short while later, Nurse Jane, a recent nursing school graduate, went into John's room with the injection. This type of injectable penicillin is a viscous liquid, so the needle was long and wide to allow for rapid movement into the muscle. Nurse Jane inserted the needle into the center of the left buttock, causing exquisite pain that shot down John's leg. Apparently, she had cut through the sciatic nerve and some small arteries, causing internal bleeding in the gluteus maximus muscle. To compound the difficulty, John was receiving intravenous heparin, a powerful anticoagulant. He continued to bleed within the muscle for several days until the area became swollen, reddened, and hard as stone. A general surgeon came in and opened the buttock for removal of the large blood clot that had formed from five days of uncontrolled internal bleeding. The subsequent pressure against the lacerated sciatic nerve caused permanent severe pain and disability.

John's lawyer discovered during the deposition questioning that Nurse Jane had graduated from nursing college only six months before the incident and that this was the first time she had ever performed an intramuscular injection. If John had asked the right questions beforehand and insisted on getting an experienced nurse to give the injection, he would likely have averted a lifetime of hurting and hobbling.

In another case, Tim J., a sixty-two-year-old man, entered a university medical center for an abdominal hernia operation. He was an asthmatic and had difficulty swallowing due to a prior stroke. Consequently, he had a tendency to choke on his food, so someone had to monitor him during meals.

One day, the nurse left Tim alone after giving him his lunch tray, and, as should have been anticipated, he started to have a nonstop coughing fit because of a small amount of food stuck in his larynx. He rang the call bell and the nurse responded immediately and inserted a suction catheter into his throat while keeping him in a sitting-up position. This was the wrong move. The nurse should have laid him supine with his neck extended to maximize the airway and called for emergency medical intervention.

To make matters worse, the nurse continued ramming the tip of the suction catheter into Tim's throat for six minutes in an aggressive effort to dislodge and remove the food particles from the upper airway. The predictable result was that she triggered a massive lung spasm causing every air passage to close permanently and he died. Knowing that her husband was a potential choking victim, Tim's wife could have avoided this by asking the nurse to verbalize the standard emergency procedure for clearing the airway of food. She, like so many others, mistakenly assumed that any nurse would know exactly what to do in a crisis. We should be able to make that assumption, but the stark reality is that we dare not.

The Nurse's Role in Medication

As to your third interview question, the subject of medication is a topic that a nurse is required to discuss with the patient and significant others. This comes under the realm of patient teaching. Make certain that you get the nurse to explain what your medications are for and what side effects can occur. Even those who already know their drugs and side effects should ask for an explanation to make sure that the nurse knows it too. Additionally, it is necessary to find out if there should be any concerns about interactions between two or more medicines. If you find that your nurse does not specifically know the details of your medications, find out if there is a drug reference book at the nurses' station, as there should be, and say that you expect your nurse to look it up. If you are not satisfied with the nurse's response, then it is time to be concerned about the person who may become the first line of defense for you or your loved one.

The Nurse as Advocate

Concerning your fourth interview question, the primary function of every nurse is to be the patient's advocate. Thus the issue as to what the nurse would do if one of the doctors or practitioners wrote a harmful order determines whether you can count on the nurse to be an effective promoter of your health. Repeatedly I review cases in which nurses did nothing when a patient needed medical attention and was not getting it or stood by while an intern or a medical student pushed the wrong medication. If I have to sleep in a hospital bed, I want a nurse who will guard me from some educated arrogant fool who is resolute to trying a bizarre medical experiment.

For a case in point, back in 1986, while working the night shift as a nurse in the intensive care unit at a community hospital in the Bronx, I was caring for a female in her mid-fifties who was receiving abdominal dialysis for kidney failure. In addition, she had liver cirrhosis with ascites (fluid collection in the abdominal cavity). An intern was on duty with me.

At 3 A.M. he wrote out several lines on an order sheet and handed it to me saying, "I expect you to carry out these instructions as soon as possible."

I looked at the paper in disbelief. The intern had written, "After the dialysate solution drains from the patient's abdomen, hang the drainage bag from the IV pole and administer solution to the patient intravenously at one hundred ccs per hour." I looked at the doctor and asked, "Is this a joke?"

"No, I'm serious."

"Why would you write such a bizarre order?"

"The patient is low on protein and I want her to receive her own protein."

I reminded him that the solution in which the protein was floating is lethal when administered intravenously. He told me to stand aside so he could do it himself. I couldn't believe it and told the doctor that I simply could not let him do that and barred his way. He just turned and left the unit in a huff. I immediately notified every person in the hospital hierarchy. I assume that the chief of medicine promptly removed that doctor because I never saw him again.

How the Nurse Can Prevent Falls and Bedsores

The last two questions asking what the nurse would do to prevent falls and bedsores are crucial matters in that there are several risk factors pertaining to both of those common life-threatening incidents. The nurse must identify the risk factors and devise a plan of care designed to prevent such occurrences. Moreover, we cannot leave prevention to staff members alone. The consumers must participate in an open dialogue with staff pertaining to the risks and care plans. The nursing and medical personnel, on the other hand, have an obligation to welcome and encourage such dialogue. There is a great deal more discussion on these areas in Chapters 4 and 5.

Who Manages the Nurses?

Returning to the primary questions of how nursing personnel manage their floors, there is clearly a possibility of discovering that a primary nurse is not up to speed on various important aspects of your care. Therefore, it is important to identify all the supervisors and learn how to summon them to register a concern or complaint. The management structure of nursing departments has gone through some theoretical model changes during the past thirty years. In practice, however, things are still the same. At first, there was a head nurse or charge nurse for each unit, with one or more supervisors in charge of the entire hospital. Now we call them nurse managers and assistant nurse managers during the day shift, and on evenings and nights we revert back, for the most part, to charge nurses and supervisors. Regardless of the title, the functions remain the same. The important consideration for the patient and family is simply to identify those who are accountable and who will respond to grievances.

Nurse-to-Patient Ratio

The next two questions, regarding the nurse-to-patient ratio and the acuity of other patients who share the same nurse, will identify how much attention the patient is going to get. Nurses measure acuity in terms of how much assistance a person needs in carrying out activities of daily living, such as eating, toileting, and personal hygiene, and how much skilled nursing time is needed to provide medical treatments and medications. There are actually five levels in standard measurements of acuity that determine how many patients a nurse can reasonably handle, assuming all the patients are at the same level. The fact that on a typical floor nurses usually have a mixture of all levels complicates this calculation. Additionally, over the past two decades, patients have been surviving longer on life support, and their doctors are moving them out of the intensive care units onto regular floors. Thus you will find a larger of percentage of artificially ventilated people on the regular floors. This formerly unacceptable practice has become a standard.

At any rate, it is difficult to determine with any precision what an acceptable nurse-to-patient ratio should be because acuity can change drastically from one moment to the next. Nonetheless, in areas where nursing shortages are acute, the dangerous levels become obvious.

To simplify the discussion of acuity, I shall identify three general levels: high, medium, and low. High acuity would identify someone who is ventilator dependent with intravenous lines, drainage tubes, and/or catheters and who may require heart monitoring by telemetry or may have an open wound. Moreover, anyone who needs total care for activities of daily living (ADLs) falls in this category.

Medium acuity defines a person who has all or some of the lines and tubes of the high-acuity patient but is not life-support dependent and does not need the heart monitor. A patient with open wounds is also included. These folks would need partial assistance with ADLs.

Finally, low acuity pertains to those who are ambulatory and independent with ADLs. They only need minimal supervision, provision of medication and treatments, and teaching.

Staffing levels in New York, Florida, Ohio, California, Texas, and South Carolina, to name a few states, are becoming dangerously low. It is common to find a floor with forty patients relying on three nurses where the acuity mix is 20 percent high, 60 percent medium, and 20 percent low. One would also find five or six life-support dependent individuals among the high-acuity group. This is dangerous, unacceptable, and commonplace. The irony is that through this threatening nursing shortage there is no shortage of nurses. There is only a shortage of nurses willing to work in hospitals. Considering their plight, this revelation should not astonish or astound anyone. Nurses work with their minds, their hearts, and their backs. They are accountable to a slew of bosses, regulators, doctors, patients, and family members in being required to anticipate and provide the needs of patients. The workload is often cruel, and there is the added pleasure of forced overtime turning an eight-hour shift into sixteen. At the end of the day, they have to worry about lawyers dragging them into court as defendants or nonparty witnesses.

Generally speaking, these shortages have been running in cycles, since more than half the workforce are married women providing secondary family incomes. During prosperous times with less general unemployment, nurses leave the workforce in droves. During recessions with high unemployment, some nurses tend to come back. The difference now is that the baby boomers are getting older with no replacements, so the available human pool is shrinking. This, coupled with the fact that we baby boomers are also going to load up the hospitals as patients in the coming years, makes the future safety of hospital services look bleak with half the nurses and twice the number of patients.

There are both short- and long-term solutions to these perils. The short-term resolution requires family participation. If your loved one is on a floor with three nurses, two nursing assistants, and forty-eight patients with the acuity mix as described previously, you have two choices. You can complain to the supervisor, or you can volunteer to participate in the care of the person for whom you are concerned. If you complain, the supervisor is likely to respond with, "I'm only a supervisor. I am not a magician." In reality, nursing supervisors spend most of their time finding nurses to work for the next shift because the prescheduled staffing levels are appallingly dangerous.

Thus if you volunteer, you will make a huge difference in keeping the patient out of harm's way. In tandem, the hospital management must do away with strict enforcement of visiting hours for family members who want to conduct a round-the-clock vigil to provide one-to-one care. Certainly, we have a right to expect full and safe service for the enormous amounts of money we pay for hospital coverage. However, the immediate concern is the safety of our family and close friends.

In the long term, on the other hand, solutions are possible but more difficult. The relief of some of the endemic problems facing nurses in hospitals requires a willingness on the part of hospital executives to acknowledge that such problems exist. Then they need to look at options like nursing program scholarships and recruitment of foreign nurses. Regarding the latter, we need some changes in federal immigration law to streamline the process of granting work visas to registered nurses from certain English-speaking countries. There also has to be a more equitable distribution of the corporate revenue of hospitals. The chief executive who makes half a million dollars per year with a cadre of executives each drawing six-figure incomes cannot justify saying that the hospital is unable to pay recruitment fees and expenses to bring nurses in from other areas. At the risk of earning the wrath and ire of hospital executives, I feel strongly that there should be a shift of some of the cash from executives' pockets to the cost of hiring and retaining more nurses.

The Physicians

With regard to the medical management, the three-pronged matter as to who is the attending physician, who is writing the orders, and who are the available specialists and what are their specialties is sometimes a mystery to the patient in a teaching hospital. First, there is a distinction between private and service patients. The private patients are usually lucky enough to have a relationship with a board-certified experienced doctor who will provide personal attention. The service patient has no such connection with the attending physician. Usually having Medicaid coverage or belonging to an HMO, service patients in many cases never get to talk to the attending physicians. Medical management is usually dedicated to resident physicians-in-training, with a signed note being placed in the record showing the physician's awareness of the case.

Second, the issue of who is writing the orders becomes a hitch when you, as the patient or visitor, find out that the nurse is serving up an unfamiliar drug. When this happens, it is time to demand a conference with the attending to find out if he or she is aware of the order and approves of it. Remember that for the most part, a post-pubescent medical school graduate is deciding your fate. If your doctor recommends an invasive procedure such as a spinal tap, find out who is going to do it and how many times that person has done it before. If you are the first one, and the attending is standing there directing the moves, it need not be a harrowing experience. I have seen many first-timers do an excellent job with good teachers guiding them. However, the teaching person should be a doctor who not only has the experience of doing the procedure but also has experience teaching it. If you do not feel comfortable with such an arrangement, you have the right to request an alternate who has done it a few times before. In any event, if the patient's body is going to be the object of a lesson, the doctors have an obligation to disclose that fact beforehand.

Finally, the age of medical specialization brings the average patient into contact with a number of different specialties of medical and surgical disciplines. When there is one physician in charge who is coordinating all medical orders, seeing one or more specialists should be beneficial. On the other hand, when different services take charge and then shift the responsibility, there is no single doctor coordinating care, and that is when the problems begin. There is often duplication of services, and, worse yet, the opposite occurs, whereby each specialist thinks that the other team is going to take care of a specific problem and no one does anything.

For example, when a patient suffers a crushing injury to a leg, two teams perform surgery. The orthopedic team reduces the fracture, while the plastics group does the skin graft. The question then becomes, "Whose job is it to change the dressings after surgery to assess wound healing and clinical progress?" If each team believes it is the responsibility of the other, no one will do the dressing change and medical follow-up.

This is exactly how a man I'll call Armand lost his right leg to gangrene at one of the teaching hospitals in New York City. This forty-seven-year-old taxi driver had gotten out of his cab to change a flat tire on the westbound side of the Queens Borough Bridge. While he was pulling his spare out of the trunk, another car hit him and crushed his right leg against the cab.

Nine hours later, Armand emerged from the operating room after arduous reconstructive surgery with bone and skin grafts. Two surgical teams were involved: orthopedics and plastics. For three weeks, no one bothered to follow up to change the dressings and evaluate the leg postoperatively, despite orders specifying that only a surgeon was to provide wound care. After the two surgical teams independently diagnosed Armand with compartment syndrome, they continued to pass the responsibility to each other. Every time the nurses asked the plastic surgeons to change the dressing, they responded with, "It's not our responsibility. Call the orthopedic residents." The nurses got a similar response from the orthopedic people, telling them to "call plastics."

When one of the nurses boldly removed the dressing because of the horrific stench of rotting flesh, the orthopedic and plastic surgeons agreed that the patient needed an emergency amputation to save his life. The leg was black at the operative site, and the diagnosis was necrotizing fasciitis (gas gangrene). If Armand and his wife had understood how the medical and nursing processes were supposed to work and that the treatment was unacceptable, he would be walking on his own two legs instead of having to use a prosthesis.

In summary, there are comparative milestones by which to differentiate between a reasonably safe hospital floor and a dangerous one. Those involve distance from the nurses' stations, emergency equipment, supplies, skill level of nurses, nurse-to-patient ratios, patient acuity, and coordination of medical specialty services. The following table provides a tool for such a comparison.

How to Tell When a Hospital Floor Is Dangerous

Reasonably Safe Hospital Floor	Warning: Enter at Your Own Peril
All rooms are within earshot of a nurses' station (circular design or substations).	There is one nurses' station for the entire floor. Some rooms are not within earshot.
Emergency equipment is present and working.	Emergency equipment is missing or broken.
Each floor has what it needs.	Emergency equipment is shared with another floor.
All required supplies are on hand.	Some supplies are missing or stored elsewhere.
All call lights are answered immediately.	Call lights flash unanswered for more than two minutes.
Nurses are satisfied with staffing levels.	Nurses are filing "unsafe staffing" reports with the supervisors.
All nurses' procedure skill levels are checked.	Skill level checks are not consistently up to date.
Nurses answer interview questions.	Nurses refuse to answer questions.
The attending physician visits with the patient daily.	The attending physician rarely or never sees the patient.
The primary physician coordinates all medical care.	Medical care is fragmented—there is no coordination.

4

Hospital Trauma: Falling and Other Mishaps

EVERY HOSPITAL HAS risk assessment and fall prevention protocols, yet every hospital has patients falling out of bed, while walking, during transfer, from a chair, from the portable commode, from the toilet, from a seated position, while taking a shower, and while dressing. A great many of those accidents result in serious and sometimes fatal injuries, such as hip fractures, skull fractures, brain hemorrhage, rib fractures, and the like.

In a court case, the question of liability rests with whether the fall was preventable. Most cases are the result of negligence where the staff members dropped the patient, forgot to put up the side rails, or failed to answer the call buzzer in a timely manner. Nonetheless, given the current state of affairs, hospital personnel cannot prevent all falls.

Thus even if a nurse takes all reasonable precautions and answers the call bells immediately, the patient could still plunge to the floor and no one person is legally to blame. Yet every accident has its cause and effect, so even when there is no specific negligence according to current standards, it is socially irresponsible to accept a certain percentage of falls as inevitable. And it seems especially irresponsible if it's you or someone you love who has fallen.

Hospitals need further investigation to find out what design flaws exist or what is lacking in the patient's environment that allows a sick person to slip out of bed undetected until the staff members hear the awful sound of someone hitting the floor or crashing into one of the furnishings and/or equipment items. Motion sensor and video surveillance technology has become wireless and inexpensive. With such devices, an alarm would go off every time a patient at risk placed an arm or leg off the bed. These patients would be mostly ambulatory elderly to whom the nurses gave instructions to call for assistance before getting out of bed.

Meanwhile, if you as the patient or family member as an advocate engage the staff and express your concern about the dangers of falling, this will heighten their awareness. Likewise, hospital management can also help to reduce incidence of falling by launching education campaigns warning new patients and family members about the possibility of falling and teaching what steps to take to maintain safety. They should hand out pamphlets and put up signs in the lobby and all the corridors. Fall prevention needs to be a cooperative effort between patients, family, and hospital executives and staff.

Identifying Those at Risk

The possibility of trauma within the hospital is supposed to be a foremost concern on the minds of management and staff alike in all hospitals. Every Nursing Admission Assessment Form must contain a tool for identifying those at risk. Although the elderly are the most vulnerable, any age can be susceptible to falling.

Aside from the obvious vigil of keeping the floors free of liquid spills and loose clutter, the following are the risk factors of falling that the admitting nurse is required to look for:

confusion, agitation, or other aberrant behavior
physical impairment, such as with a history of stroke
balance impairment, as with inner ear inflammation

low blood pressure (postural hypotension)
history of fainting (syncope)
history of epilepsy
nonwalking persons of any age
visual impairment
age greater than sixty-five
frequent urge to urinate
diarrhea
history of falling
taking sedatives, hypnotics, narcotics, and the like
neurological diseases such as Parkinson's and multiple
  sclerosis

Family members need to make the nurse aware if any of these conditions exists. After such a report is made, it is vital to discuss with the nurse what the specific plan is for fall prevention. All nurses are required to write and update a care plan on their patients. Ask to see this plan. It would be interesting to see the responses if all consumers would ask the nurse to produce a copy of the care plan. The level of diligence would soar to new heights.

To start with, confusion, agitation, and other acting-out behaviors are serious management problems. Patients exhibiting such behaviors not only are prone to falling but are also at risk for hurting themselves and others by disrupting the rendering of care. This includes pulling out lines and tubes and attempting acts of violence against staff members and other patients. The patient who is obviously confused and given to bizarre and/or violent behavior is easy to identify, and there are specific prescribed actions that I shall discuss later in this chapter.

However, a more difficult problem exists with people who do not exhibit such behavior initially and become unpredictably confused at night. The elderly are especially vulnerable because they lack the ability to adjust to an unfamiliar environment. Confusion often sets in at night when the patient wakes up thinking that he or she is still at home. This often leads to the person getting out of bed without calling for help. This is particularly troublesome because nurses are often lulled into a false sense of safety from interacting with a patient who through the entire day has demonstrated lucidity and full cooperation with hospital routine. The onset of momentary confusion in such persons is unpredictable.

In the case of Esther M., she was seventy-four years old when she entered the hospital for a biopsy of a lump in her right breast. After the surgery, she was having trouble sleeping, so the doctor prescribed a mild sedative, which she took at 6 P.M. and again at 10 P.M. The night nurse made rounds regularly every hour. Although Esther was independent and ambulatory during the day, the nurse assessed her as being at moderate risk of falling due to her age being over seventy. The protocol was to keep two side rails up at night at the head of the bed and to frequently remind the patient to call for assistance before getting out of bed. About fifteen minutes after the night nurse made 1 A.M. rounds, Esther attempted to climb out of bed and fell, sustaining a fracture to her left hip.

According to current standards, the nursing staff did everything they were required to do. They made a reasonable assessment of the risk, they made rounds every hour, and they kept two of the four side rails up at night. Obviously, that was not enough to keep Esther from falling and fracturing her hip. There is a design defect in the standard. The question is, "What's missing?" The answer is surveillance. As mentioned previously, we need family involvement and consumer activism to upgrade the current standards. A standard by which the courts judge a health professional is nothing more than a consensus of like professionals opining that the injury was "unfortunate but unavoidable."

Assessing risk comes down to first observing whether an individual is prone to falling and then anticipating the likelihood that a person who is disposed to falling is going to attempt some form of movement with no one in attendance.

The question of being susceptible to falling is a matter of whether a person needs assistance with sitting up, standing, walking, transferring, and sitting in a chair or on a toilet seat. Even with those who are independent in such matters, there is also the question of balance and judgment as well as whether any conditions exist that cause fainting and/or dizziness. Those could be either an illness such as diabetes, heart block, low blood pressure, anemia, and panic attacks or side effects from medications.

A case in point is an incident involving Rachel, a thirty-two-year-old female who entered a university medical center after suffering from a leaking aneurysm in the right side of her brain. Fortunately, the neurosurgeons were able to place a clip to seal off the blood leak. However, there was some residual damage from the blood collection. The clot left Rachel with residual strokelike left-sided partial paralysis. The advantage was that she was young and responded extremely well to physical therapy. Everyone involved, including the patient and her husband, expected a near-full recovery. However, this was not to be the case. Rachel had made a lot of progress but still needed assistance to walk to the bathroom, and she had some difficulty balancing herself on the toilet.

About three weeks after surgery, one of the nurses assisted Rachel in walking to the bathroom and helped her onto the toilet. The nurse, wanting to give Rachel some privacy, said, "I'll be right outside the door if you need me."

Moments later, Rachel fell over toward her left side and slammed her head on the floor. The nurse, who remained outside the bathroom door, was unable to prevent the injury. Shortly thereafter, Rachel was in the operating room with a neurosurgeon removing the blood clot from the left side of her brain. Following this, Rachel was now dealing with partial paralysis on both sides. The chances of her future recovery became remote. This terrible scenario could have easily been avoided, but not without the patient and her family being educated in the risks and taking a proactive role in risk prevention by engaging the nursing staff in a continuous dialogue regarding safety concerns with the hemiparesis (one-sided partial paralysis).

"Mysterious" Injuries

There are injuries beyond falls to be aware of. Periodically, a patient will sustain serious injury in a hospital room and no one seems to be able to give an accounting of how it happened. A simple fall is not usually the explanation in these cases. Some of my investigations have uncovered gross incompetence with a reckless disregard for safety, while others pointed to criminal assault. Three case histories come to mind, with different explanations.

A Nurse's Aide Scared to Tell the Truth

This investigation involved Kristine D., a thirty-eight-year-old woman who had come out of surgery following removal of an ovarian cyst at a hospital in one of the New England states. She fell while a nurse's aide attempted to hoist her out of bed about three hours after she returned from the recovery room. The nurse had received postoperative orders to get Kristine "out of bed as tolerated." She then sent in the nurse's aide to get the patient out of bed.

A few minutes later, the nurse's aide was calling for help, and Kristine was on the floor. The aide said that she had assisted Kristine in standing up and that Kristine had passed out cold. Being unable to hold the patient up, the aide insisted that she had eased Kristine to the floor while holding on to her left arm.

The x-rays revealed that Kristine had a displaced fracture of the jaw with the joint dislodged from left to right. Additionally, there was bleeding from her left ear, and the CAT scan revealed a hairline fracture of her skull behind the same ear. As if that were not enough, there was also a frontal fracture of the maxilla (facial bone holding the upper teeth) and two broken front teeth. This was proof positive that there was blunt trauma in three different places about the head: front, side, and back. The story of "easing her down to the floor" certainly did not explain this. From the injuries, we knew that Kristine had taken three separate blows to the head. Only the nurse's aide could tell us exactly how this happened. She was obviously scared to tell the truth.

However, without excluding the possibility of a criminal attack, I theorized that this was a bizarre accident arising out of the nurse delegating her task to a staff member who had no idea what to do. The aide was holding an unconscious woman by one arm when she fell and first hit her face on the arm of a wooden chair. The aide, still holding Kristine by the right arm, then unintentionally swung Kristine's head into another object, hitting first the left side and then the back (or vice versa), after which she eased Kristine to the floor.

In any event, the charge nurse could have avoided Kristine's trauma by one simple action. The nurse needed to be with the patient getting out of bed after surgery for the first time because the order stated "as tolerated." This required that the nurse make an assessment to see if Kristine could endure standing up and walking. The nurse would have accomplished this by taking the blood pressure readings immediately after Kristine sat up and stood. If there had been a sudden drop in pressure as there often is after surgery, then the nurse would have to abort the attempt to get Kristine out of bed and notify the doctor. Postural hypotension is what caused Kristine to pass out.

More Than a Fall

This scenario is regarding the very sad death of Mercedes, a nineteen-year-old woman who was a patient at one of the New York State psychiatric facilities in New York City back in 1988. One of the staff members found her unconscious at the bottom of a stairwell that led to a locked ward on the second floor. An ambulance took her to a local hospital, and she died two days later without waking up. Her father hired an attorney who asked me to review the records.

The incident report stated that Mercedes had escaped from the unit and was found at the bottom of the stairs. The hospital's investigation concluded that she had fallen and sustained the fatal head injury. There was something very wrong with this assumption for three reasons. First, she was lying on her back. This is not how a person lands after tumbling down one or two flights of stairs. Even if she jumped over the banister in a suicide attempt, she could not have landed in a straight supine position.

Second, the autopsy photographs showed that Mercedes had bruises all over her body, front and back as well as her head. This could not have happened from tumbling down stairs or plummeting over the banister. Someone more than likely beat her with a blunt instrument and placed her at the bottom of the stairs so it would appear to be an accident.

Finally, the psychiatric hospital record revealed that Mercedes was in seclusion during the prior evening for "acting abusively toward staff." Then she mysteriously "disappeared." Putting these facts together gives cause to suspect foul play. It was surprising to read in the autopsy report that the medical examiner ruled that the death was an accident rather than a homicide.

Staff Avoiding Blame

This case is about Merryl B., a seventy-nine-year-old woman who suffered a right lower leg spiral fracture in a Midwest hospital. There was no documented incident in the hospital record consistent with such a fracture.

While reviewing the record, I found a nurse's note stating that while being transferred from the stretcher to her regular hospital bed after coming back from the physical therapy unit, Merryl screamed in pain and was complaining of her leg hurting ever since. After conferring with an orthopedic surgeon, we concluded that the nature of the fracture indicated that she had fallen between the stretcher and the bed, with her foot caught in the side rail, and had twisted her leg suddenly and forcefully.

The two nurses apparently did not want to take the heat for this obvious negligence and conspired to put Merryl back in bed and just note that she inexplicably started screaming and shouting obscenities. This was a clever ruse since Merryl had been confused and agitated before and was verbally abusive. They figured that if there were an injury, other staff members would discover it days later, and the patient would not remember when it occurred and/or would not be a credible witness.

The scheme worked out as planned. The staff were accustomed to Merryl's screaming, and no one checked her complaint until a physical therapist found that there was a real problem with the leg three days after the incident.

What could these three women's families have done? It is hard if not impossible to be present every second of your loved one's hospital stay. Rather, these scenarios show that you need to make a careful assessment of the environment and personnel before leaving him or her behind in a hospital.

How to Prevent Falls and Injuries

Nurses are required without exception to prepare a care plan for all new patients. Moreover, they must also review and update these plans daily. Many nonmedical people think of nursing as a task-oriented menial and subservient job. But nursing is in fact a health science with an independent body of knowledge based on academic methodical research conducted at major universities throughout the world. One major benefit of this is that nurses can independently diagnose and treat human responses to existing and potential health problems.

Accordingly, a nurse has to figure out how a patient is likely to respond to biological and psychological changes, social interactions, and environmental influences. In so doing, nurses must learn to calculate the probability of untoward events—accidents—for each patient. They must then plan for and implement ways to prevent occurrences.

In keeping with this form of accountability, nursing leaders have devised a standard tool for calculating the level of risk of falling and implementing protocols for prevention. This tool takes each of the risk factors listed above and assigns a numerical value. The nurse adds the values present, and the total determines whether the risk is low, moderate, or high. The actual numbers vary from one institution to another and are not important because they all translate to the three basic levels of risk.

Patients who are considered low risk can still fall and get hurt, and they often do. Perhaps because a patient is rated low risk, the staff conclude that there is no risk, which actually increases the likelihood of an accident because there is less vigilance with preventive measures. The standard prevention protocols, which are inadequate, are as follows:

- Teach the patient about the dangers of falling and to call for assistance before attempting to get out of bed.
- Keep the side rails up at the head of the bed.
- Keep the call bell within reach.
- Provide immediate response to calls for assistance.
- Keep urinals and bedpans within reach.
- Keep water and other fluids within reach.
- Keep other personal items within reach.
- Conduct pain assessments and take action to relieve discomfort.
- Make rounds at night at least once per hour to check.

The nurses actually have to do all of these things. If they disregard any of these items, there is a potential for disaster. And even when they overlook nothing, people still fall and sustain serious injury. As said before, the missing element is continuous monitoring. There are advertisements on the Internet offering wide scanning wireless video surveillance cameras that transmit the images to a desktop computer. The retail price is about $80 each for the complete kit. A hospital with five hundred beds would need to purchase about two hundred kits for a total cost of $16,000 less volume discounts. The desktop computers at the nurses' station could carry multiple images of those rooms under observation. Even at four times the price, it would be a small amount to pay for added patient safety.

Moderate risk involves people who seem to be lucid and oriented to person, place, and time but have some physical impairment predisposing them to falls. Additionally, moderate risk could pertain to someone who has no physical impairment but is slightly confused at times (there are no absolutes in calculating risk). In any event, the four side rails should remain up at all times, and there should be a requirement for more frequent bed checks. The rest of the items remain the same. These people should also be no more than five doors away from the nurses' station.

High-risk individuals are likely to fall or harm themselves or others unless constantly monitored. These people are always confused and/or continuously uncooperative. Sometimes there is a risk of violent or suicidal behavior. High-risk patients generally require a person within arm's length at all times. The charge nurse usually accomplishes this by assigning a nurse's aide to sit with the patient and provide custodial care. Sometimes various forms of restraints are necessary, especially if there is a risk of a combative patient assaulting the sitter. Often, combative behavior results from the patient being frightened and not understanding what is going on. Such patients believe that they are fighting for their lives. The staff members must be educated to this point and refrain from reacting with anger or disdain. Having a family member remain with the patient whenever possible helps to alleviate much of the fear factor because this is someone with whom the patient is familiar. It does not always work but it can be most helpful, and as my Jewish mother always said, "It couldn't hurt."

Patients or family members should always ask the nurse to state what risk level he or she has assigned. It is also advisable to ask the nurse to provide a copy of the fall prevention care plan. Additionally, for those who wish to engage in community activism, attend the next community board meeting at your hospital and lobby for more video surveillance. If the hospital is severely strapped for cash (as many are), then it would be most helpful to plan a fund-raising drive to pay for such equipment.

Restraints

The subject of restraints always comes up with the discussion of preventing falls in high-risk patients. There have been injuries related to the misuse of restraints. Falls and other injuries resulting from ripping out items such as urinary bladder catheters are also sometimes related to the failure to apply restraints or to their improper application. To protect family and friends while in the hospital you need to learn about restraints and their appropriate use. The restraints currently in use are four side rails, vest restraints (e.g., Poseys), wrist restraints, and leg restraints.

Side Rails

Side rails are self-explanatory. Current standards require viewing side rails as a restraint because they restrict the patient's physical freedom.

Vest Restraints

The vest restraint is mostly for elderly patients who are likely to attempt to get out of bed but are not constantly trying to do so. The proper application for most brands requires putting it on like donning a clothing vest and crisscrossing the ends at the front. The nurse then ties the straps together under the bed. All nursing personnel learn two overriding principles. Vest restraints are dangerous when not applied correctly or when used as a substitute for patient monitoring.

I have recently reviewed one case from the Southwest in which a nurse found an elderly male patient strangled in a vest restraint. The vest was on backward, which brought the neckline up to the patient's throat. The poor soul, while trying to wriggle out of it, virtually hanged himself. In many other cases, unmonitored patients had fallen on the floor or had wandered off while the vest remained on the bed still tied.

Wrist Restraints

Wrist restraints are for keeping the patient from pulling on intravenous lines and tubes. Such occurrences have disastrous effects, especially with lines that have been inserted into the chest wall. Bladder catheters have water-inflated balloons on the internal end to keep them from slipping out. When yanked out suddenly, they cause internal damage to the urinary sphincter. In men, the damage is much worse because the balloon is pulled internally through the length of the penis. So it is crucial to prevent this from occurring. The downside is that wrist restraints can also cause injury when not applied properly or the wrong type of material is used. Current regulations forbid the use of items like gauze rolls or orthopedic stocking materials because they can cut off circulation and cause either nerve damage resulting in paralysis or gangrene resulting in amputation. The proper item is a wristband designed to maintain a comfortable space between the material and the skin and that remains in place with a Velcro fastener. The strap that restricts movement of the forearm ties to a loop that attaches to the wristband. Thus when patients pull on it (and they always do), they cannot cut off circulation to the hand. Most states have laws that prohibit the use of any other material.

Every hospital also has rules that require releasing the arms from restraints one at a time to allow full range of motion at least once every hour. Every nurse is required to maintain a restraint documentation record, and a doctor's order is required within one hour of the nurse's decision to apply such a measure. Hospitals also require that the doctors periodically renew and review such orders.

Leg Restraints

Leg restraints are the same shape as wrist restraints, only larger. Restraining all four limbs is only for extreme situations when dealing with a patient who is wildly combative. It is for short-term use only, and the same rules apply with regard to range of motion. To make sure that every limb receives full range of motion every hour, the nurse has to free one every fifteen minutes. In most such cases, the physician will order some form of sedation. When the medication takes effect, usually the nurse can remove the leg restraints.

What You Can Do

Restraints are sometimes necessary, but nurses must apply them only as a last resort. Nurses are obliged to closely monitor the situation and try all other means to maintain safety, including a one-to-one sitter. Family members can be extremely helpful if they have the time and dedication. If you discover that the nurses and doctors have placed your loved one in restraints, ask to review the pertinent policies and procedures, and check to see if the nurses are following them. Never presuppose that everyone is going to do what is required at all times. Reality just does not work that way.

Here is what you can do to assure that the restraints achieve the desired goal without accidental complications:

- Ask the nurse to explain the rationale for using the restraints.
- Ask for a copy of the written policy and procedure pertaining to the particular restraint being used.
- Go over the requirements with the unit charge nurse.
- Stay with the patient as much as possible.
- Give frequent loving reassurance even if the patient does not appear to understand.

The health-care system cannot keep all patients safe from injurious accidents. New laws and regulations to implement improvements can help, but the only way to immediately ensure a safe hospital stay is for you, the consumer, to take control and safeguard yourself and your loved ones. You can do this as follows:

1. Demand the right to see all the care plans related to safety and accident prevention.

2. Review those plans with the nurses.

3. Take the opportunity to voice approval or recommend alternatives.

The nurses should feel obliged to include the patients and significant others in establishing such plans of care.

How to Prevent Falling and Other Mishaps

- Review the checklist of risk factors (see "Identifying Those at Risk") as soon as you have arrived at the hospital.
- If you have identified that you or your loved one is at risk of falling, speak to the admitting nurse and get agreement as to the level of risk that exists (low, moderate, or high).
- Review the fall prevention protocol or care plan with the admitting nurse (see "How to Prevent Falls and Injuries").
- Check the room and the patient each time you visit, and immediately report any deviations from the protocol, such as side rails down, call bell not in reach, and so on.
- If your loved one is agitated or confused, make sure that the patient is never left alone. Insist on one-to-one service (a nurse's aide at the bedside at all times).
- If your loved one is in restraints, make certain that the nurses are documenting the release of each limb as required.
- Maximize surveillance:
  - Stay with your loved one as much as possible.
  - Request transfer to a bed as near to the nurses' station as possible.
  - Request video surveillance if available.

5

Preventing Mishaps in the Intensive Care Units

INTENSIVE CARE IS, without a doubt, the scariest part of any hospital. Some of the more recently constructed intensive care units (ICUs) look like a scene in a science fiction movie, with all the electronic monitoring devices and life-support machines. Most people who have to stay in such places are critically ill and need a lot more than a regular hospital floor can provide. Part of dealing with catastrophic illness is the intimidating effect of the high-technology machines. Nurses and physicians usually connect critically ill patients to such equipment by attaching wires to the skin and inserting tubes into various parts of the anatomy. The sights and sounds of all this will understandably generate feelings of apprehension and may prevent you from being able to scrutinize the services objectively. This feeling of being overwhelmed is simply a response to finding yourself in unfamiliar territory. In order to avoid being intimidated and be able to evaluate the quality of the services being provided, it is essential to learn a few basic facts about the equipment, multiple drug administration, blood transfusion, dialysis, and staffing in critical care for adults, children (pediatrics), and newborn infants (neonates).

Although we can also find the same high-tech devices and complications on regular floors, we shall explore those in this chapter because they are more common in the critical care areas. We shall also look at a strange phenomenon called ICU psychosis, which is a common reaction to all the elements of critical care. Finally, in the last segment of this chapter, we will look into standing orders, appropriate staffing levels, and the code (cardiopulmonary resuscitation).

What You Need to Know About Wires and Tubes

The wires adhere to the chest skin surface with sticky pads for monitoring the heart rate and rhythm. Sometimes you will find multiple wires attached to the scalp and hooked up to an electroencephalograph. This measures brain wave patterns. These monitoring systems are benign and do not directly cause any complications. However, the monitor screen is only as good as the person who is watching it. If no one is keeping an eye on it, then it is useless. Therefore, when you arrive on the unit, your first question should be, "Who is watching the monitors?" Although these electronic gadgets all have alarm systems, many staff members learn to ignore them because they often go off for no reason. The danger associated with cardiac monitors is the possibility that a potentially lethal heart rhythm and/or rate would appear on the display and no one would notice.

There are six different functions for the various-sized plastic tubes, which are the same for infants and children as for adults: infusion, blood and blood product transfusion, feeding, drainage, monitoring, and breathing. We'll look at each of these, go over the most common threatening complications associated with each, and learn how to prevent permanent damage. Although some complications cannot be avoided, most often the difference between a complication resulting in permanent injury or not depends upon how the nurses and doctors respond—with the nurses being the first line of defense.

Infusion Lines

The infusion lines deliver fluids, minerals, and nutrition directly into the blood vessels. Most intravenous (IV) lines are put in an arm (peripheral intravenous lines), but some go directly into the chest wall (central intravenous lines). One common problem is when a peripheral intravenous line infiltrates, meaning the vein ruptures and the intravenous liquids infuse into the surrounding tissues. This causes massive swelling and, if it continues, leads to a chronic ulceration. Some intravenous fluids are caustic, and infiltration results in almost immediate sloughing and third-degree burns. It is important to check the infusion entry site for swelling, redness, and heat. If any of these problems exist, a registered nurse must respond by closing off the line and removing it. If this does not happen within three minutes, dial the operator and page the nursing supervisor. This is an urgent matter, and the nurses must treat it as such.

I have reviewed hundreds of cases in which patients incurred third-degree burns and permanent damage to tendons and nerves, resulting in terrible scars, due to the nurses' failure to take immediate action with an infiltrated intravenous line. One such case was a newborn boy named Johnny. As is normally the case, one of the neonatal ICU nurses started an intravenous line in the baby's right foot. The intravenous fluid infiltrated and infused into the soft tissues of the foot for about four hours. Apparently, the nurse responsible for making hourly assessments of the intravenous site failed to do so. By making frequent observations, the nurse would have noticed that the child's foot was growing larger. The result was the equivalent of a third-degree burn and a permanent clubbing deformity.

Moreover, it is especially important to note that Johnny's mother was present the whole time. If she had known about the possibility of swelling caused by infiltration, she would have been able to get the nurse to intercede or summon the supervisor to take action. The greatest danger to being hospitalized is being uninformed while relying totally on the "flawless" performance of the professional and ancillary staff.

Blood Transfusions

Blood transfusions, which have always been somewhat chancy, have become a higher risk because of hepatitis and AIDS. Blood bank intake personnel are supposed to screen all blood donors for AIDS and hepatitis. The reality is that they do not always accomplish that. There have been thousands of AIDS and hepatitis victims from tainted blood. The cost of testing all the blood was so high that it was apparently cheaper to pay off a few lawsuits than screen all the incoming blood. The reality about blood banks is that they pay for most of the blood they receive. People who sell their blood are usually destitute intravenous drug abusers. This is an extremely high-risk population, and that makes blood transfusion dangerous. Current federal law requires labeling blood that identifies every purchased unit. Unless you or your loved one is getting an emergency transfusion, you should accept such blood only if there is no alternative.

If you want to donate blood directly to a family member or friend, you need to ask if the hospital blood bank has the ability to type, cross-match, and process your blood and give it to the intended recipient. Most local hospitals do not have that capability. They get their supply from a central blood bank, and your donation would go into the general stock.

Another alternative to accepting the risk of receiving tainted blood is autotransfusion. If you are planning elective surgery, you can donate blood to yourself if your hospital has such a program. In those places, the hospital will process your blood and keep it for your exclusive use. If you find yourself in a conversation with a surgeon about elective surgery, remember to ask about autotransfusion.

The other area of blood transfusion risk is mismatched blood. The results could be lethal, so the nurses must take great care in making certain that the blood type matches. Each blood transfusion unit has a serial number and the blood type. The standard procedure is for two nurses to check that the serial number on the bag matches the one on the ticket. They will also check the blood type against what is on the chart. The symptoms of blood reaction are low-grade fever and chills. This is a medical emergency, so if you happen to be the one who discovers it, get the nurse. You must get an immediate response. The nurse must first turn off the transfusion and then summon the doctor. The doctor must also respond immediately. He or she will prescribe certain drugs depending on the severity of the reaction.

Feeding Tubes

Feeding tubes are either inserted through the nose or surgically placed through the abdominal wall and are usually attached to a bag through a pump. There are two possible dangers with tube feeding: (1) The stomach can become overloaded, making the person vomit. This poses a threat because the person can inhale the vomit into the lungs. (2) The liquid nutrition often causes diarrhea, which can, in turn, cause skin excoriation and bedsores.

Such complications lead to permanent damage when nurses fail to properly regulate the feeding tube flow rate and fail to respond immediately to control the diarrhea. Meticulous nursing care is the only way to avoid these complications.

To prevent overload, nurses must check the amount of fluid in the stomach by placing a large syringe into the end of the feeding tube and drawing back on the plunger. This will remove the stomach contents so the nurse can measure the amount.

Diarrhea is usually treated by adjusting the formula and administering a drug that slows down the bowel action.

What questions to ask the nurse and how to ask them. Asking questions is one of the most important ways to prevent complications. However, you should be aware that you are about to speak to a person who is likely to be stressed out with an overwhelming workload. If you approach in a threatening, mistrustful, or accusatory manner, you will probably not get the answer you need. Here are the recommended questions:

- Why are you pumping the feeding at the current rate?
- I am worried that the patient's stomach will get overloaded. How will you prevent that?

- What plan do you have to prevent diarrhea?
- If there is diarrhea, how will you eliminate this problem while maintaining skin integrity?

Drainage Tubes

The purpose of drainage tubes is to remove body fluids from the bladder, kidneys, stomach, bile duct, and/or surgical site.

Bladder catheters. The bladder catheters either hang from the urinary opening or protrude through the abdomen from surgical placement. These pose a significant risk of infection because the tubes provide a conduit for skin surface bacteria and viruses to enter the bladder. There is also the possibility of injury because the catheters remain in the bladder with fluid-filled balloons attached to the indwelling tip. This type of injury was covered in the section about restraints in Chapter 4. Nurses are educated to be aware of these latent problems and provide preventive measures that include using disinfectant solu-

Date	Problem Identification (Nursing Diagnosis)	Goals	Planned Intervention	Follow-up and Outcome
10/22/02	Risk of urinary tract infection due to indwelling bladder catheter (Foley).	No urinary tract infection.	Catheter care with antibacterial soap, water, and application of Betadine ointment at meatus every 8 hours.	10/25/02 Urine clear and yellow. No sign of infection.
10/22/02	Risk of urinary tract injury due to presence of bladder catheter.	No urinary tract injury.	Keep catheter secured to inner thigh with tape. Teach patient that catheter can cause urge to urinate and be a source of irritation. Remind patient periodically that the catheter is there.	10/25/02 Catheter intact. No sign of injury.

tion for catheter care and taping the catheter to the leg to prevent accidental pulling.

Additionally, it is important to realize that the presence of a bladder catheter can be very irritating, causing the constant feeling of having to urinate. There is often a risk of critically ill patients becoming confused and yanking out the tube to get rid of the source of irritation. I have reviewed a number of cases resulting in major damage to the urinary tract requiring a permanent urine tube placed through the lower abdominal wall. To nurses and physicians, bladder catheters are commonplace. Thus you would increase your safety if you remind them of the measures to prevent injury. The best way to do this is to ask to see the nursing care plan. It should look something like the sample on the facing page.

Asking nurses to show and go over their care plans with you as a patient or family member may throw them off balance and cause a negative response because they are not accustomed to client scrutiny. The best way to respond to such a reaction is to reassure the nurse, "I am not questioning your competence, but I am going to exercise my right to participate in my care [the care of my husband, wife, father, mother, sister, brother, child, etc.]. Therefore, I must go over the nursing care plan for preventing the common complications of bladder catheters." (Nurses commonly use the term Foley catheters.)

Kidney catheters. Continuing with drainage tubes, the kidney catheters hang out of the lower left and/or right side of the trunk. These are trickier than bladder catheters because they have no balloons to hold them in. They pose a greater threat because there is the possibility of kidney infection and damage from urinary obstruction if the tube becomes kinked. Thus the doctor has to anchor the kidney catheter to the skin with stitches near the insertion site, and the area must remain clean and as germ-free as possible. These tubes are about as wide as coffee stirrers, and I have too often found them lying in the bed or on the floor. When kidney catheters dislodge, the nurse must regard it as an emergency and immediately notify the urologist. Once again, you as the patient or family member need to be aware of this in case there is no follow-through from the staff. Consequently, if you have a loved one with a kidney tube, check it every time you go for a visit to see if it is still attached. If you discover that it has dislodged, you must ask the nurse the following questions:

- Did you report it to the doctor?
- Did the doctor respond?
- What is the doctor doing about it?

Remember that this is a medical emergency. If the urologist is not responding accordingly, you have to start complaining to administration, and you cannot stop until the doctor comes and takes the necessary action.

Internal Monitoring Tubes and Hospital-Induced Anemia

These tubes are invasive, meaning that doctors have to insert them into certain arteries and large veins to monitor the blood pressure and the dynamics of the blood flow through the heart and lungs. Monitoring blood pressure in the arteries requires that a catheter be placed in one of the arteries of the wrist, arm, or leg. The nurse or doctor attaches this catheter to a fluid-filled bag via a plastic tube and keeps it under high pressure to prevent hemorrhage. The nurses and doctors also use these catheters to obtain blood samples for testing. While on one hand it is good to avoid multiple needle sticks for blood samples, this presents a high risk for hospital-induced anemia (or iatrogenic anemia, as health-care professionals sometimes call it) because the nurse or doctor must allow some of the blood to flow out in order to avoid testing a mixture of blood and intravenous fluid. Hospital-induced anemia is a major problem among the critically ill. ICU patients require many blood tests every eight hours. Those with arterial lines have about 20 cc of blood removed every three to four hours for blood gas analysis and arterial line calibration. The result of all this is that hospital personnel are draining too much blood from critically ill people. One would almost think that medieval bloodletting was still in vogue. Hospital-induced anemia is a serious problem because the victims are already weak and cannot afford such blood loss. The result of this kind of anemia is having insufficient amounts of oxygen circulating to the vital organs, resulting in damage to the brain, heart, lungs, liver, and kidneys. This condition also slows healing of surgical wounds and worsens problems associated with poor circulation.

The amazingly sad thing about hospital-induced anemia is that medical researchers have recognized it in the medical literature for at least the past twenty years. The solution is simply to use smaller test tubes. Laboratory personnel don't need large blood samples—they only use about 10 percent of the blood drawn for testing. The other 90 percent winds up as medical waste. The only way to protect the patient from this situation is to tell the charge nurse that you are aware of the possibility of too much blood being drawn for testing and you would like to monitor the situation. The more that patients and family members remind nurses of the risk of damaging events, the more diligent nurses are likely to become in preventing them. If you or a loved one has an arterial or central venous line from which blood is to be drawn for testing, you might want to tell the nurse that you have been reading about hospital-induced anemia (you might want to show your copy of this book) and have a couple of questions. Here is what you might ask:

- How much blood do you intend to draw out to flush the line for each test?
- Is it possible to group all the routine blood tests at specific times to reduce the amount of blood loss for flushing the line?
- How much blood will you draw out for test samples?
- Wouldn't the smaller pediatric (child-size) test tubes provide enough of a sample?
- Are you going to monitor the blood test results for any signs of anemia?

Hospital-induced anemia was the problem with Maria P., a sixty-eight-year-old who entered the hospital for a gall bladder removal. She went to the surgical ICU after surgery and stayed there for twelve days for control of diabetes, high blood pressure, and congestive heart failure. The day that the doctors transferred Maria to the step-down unit, she went into respiratory crisis and cardiac arrest. The nurses and physicians responded within seconds, and they stabilized her within three minutes of the arrest. Although her heart and lungs were functioning, they could not awaken her. She had brain damage beyond repair and remained in a coma for eight months before she died.

The family's attorney asked me to investigate why there was so much brain damage after the textbook performance in reviving the patient. This was indeed a fascinating mystery. The answer was in the gradual and unnoticed deterioration in the blood count of red blood cells, hemoglobin, and hematocrit. She had significant blood loss anemia, but there was no record of any active bleeding, and there was no problem maintaining her blood pressure. Finally, having written about hospital-induced anemia in my master's thesis back in 1988, I started to calculate the amount of blood lost to the number of blood tests and arterial line calibrations Maria had had. It turned out that the nurses and physicians were unwittingly draining about 250 milliliters of blood from the patient every day for twelve days. In healthy adults, this would not have been significant, but Maria's ailing body was unable to compensate. Thus she became anemic, and her heart, brain, lungs, and other vital organs lacked sufficient oxygen. Taking samples with smaller tubes that are already available on all pediatric floors and units could have prevented this tragedy.

Heart Flow Monitors

The most commonly used set of tubes for heart flow monitoring is the Swan-Ganz catheter. This device also allows for monitoring the blood pressure in the pulmonary artery and measuring the pumping effectiveness of the heart (cardiac output). This device goes into one of the main veins leading into the heart (superior or inferior vena cava) through the neck or under the collarbone (clavicle).

After the procedure, a chest x-ray is always required to make sure that the catheter is in the right place. Following that, the most significant hazards are fluid overload and infection. The risk of fluid overload is due to the fact that with the Swan-Ganz there is a central intravenous line in addition to whatever other IV lines the doctors and nurses have established. When there are three or four IVs, the nurses have to monitor the infusions carefully to prevent overload. This is especially dangerous if the patient has congestive heart failure, because the additional fluid can back up into the lungs and cause internal drowning.

The possibility of infection looms large because there is a foreign body—the tube—connecting the outside world to the sterile heart chambers. This tube penetrates all protective barriers against invading microorganisms. Thus the nurses have to maintain a sterile dressing over the insertion site and clean the area daily using a sterile technique. They must also maintain sterility whenever they open or penetrate the system. Understanding that they cannot always prevent infection despite best efforts, the nurses' response to the signs and symptoms of catheter contamination is critical. The strongest signs would be fever and chills. Redness at the insertion site is also a cause for concern. If you see any of these signs, be sure the nurses are aware of them and that they immediately contact the on-call physician for medical orders. The physician should respond by ordering blood, urine, and sputum cultures. If the doctor determines that the catheter is the source of infection, he or she must remove it, insert a new one (if it is still medically necessary), and order one or more intravenous antibiotics in accordance with the culture and sensitivity report (the report must show that the bug is not resistant to the antibiotic).

Breathing Tubes

The act of connecting most people to ventilator machines requires that a plastic tube be placed in the upper airway (endotracheal tube). The presence of the throat tube places the patient at high risk for internal pressure ulceration of the mouth and throat and for lung infection. The prevention of this complication requires meticulous nursing care. The tube has an internal balloon, which, when inflated, anchors the device in the windpipe (trachea). This causes pressure and must be relieved every eight hours for a few minutes. The nurse has to be careful not to allow the tube to dislodge during this procedure. There is also pressure against the inside of the mouth and the tongue. Thus the nurse has to reposition the outer portion of the tube every eight hours.

Additionally, when a person has to remain connected to a breathing tube for a long period or when there is swelling in the upper windpipe, a surgeon makes a hole in the throat (tracheostomy) and connects the breathing tube to the respirator through this opening.

Preventing lung infection is a more difficult task. The human airway has a number of natural safeguards to prevent lung infection. The first line of defense is the structure of the throat that traps dust particles and droplets. This is a highly effective barrier to infection. The endotracheal or tracheostomy tube bypasses this structure and allows dust and contaminated droplets to enter directly into the lower airways. This brings us to a discussion about sputum. I know that this particular subject is disgusting, but it is the only way for you to know if your loved one is suffering from a potential lethal lung infection, so you will need to get past your initial revulsion. All too often, nurses will go about their business and not notice the signs of respiratory system deterioration. Therefore, if you have a family member or close friend on a respirator in the ICU, you will need to be able to monitor changes in the color and consistency of the lung secretions. Then you will know whether to alert the nurses and doctors that something looks wrong and demand to know what they are going to do about it. You will be able to see the sputum because the exhaled air expels it into the clear plastic tubing that attaches the patient's airway to the breathing machine. The table on the facing page explains what to look for and what to do about it.

Although infection is not always avoidable, nurses are required to perform certain services working toward a goal of keeping the airway free of infection. This requires suctioning as needed with lavage (squirting three milliliters of saline into the airway tube for cleansing the airway and loosening the dried secretions). If the patient sounds congested with raspy breathing noises, get the nurse immediately and demand that he or she suction the patient. There is no substitute for aggressive meticulous nursing care.

How to Spot Respiratory Problems

Color	Consistency	Odor	Comment
Clear	Thin	None	Within normal limits.
Clear	Thick	None	Within normal limits.
White	Thin	None	Within normal limits.
White	Thick	None	First sign of problem—might be due to dehydration.
Yellow	Thick	None to slight	Upper respiratory infection—get the nurse and find out what the treatment plan is.
Yellow to green	Thick	Slight	Infection is getting worse—the treatment plan is not working. Find out what they are doing about it.
Cream colored	Thick	Moderate	This is purulence (pus) coming from the lungs. Ask the doctor if there is an infectious disease consultant on the case. If not, make a demand for one.
Coffee colored	Thick and chunky	Foul	This is likely a dangerous deep lung infection with possible gangrene. Insist on a detailed explanation of the interventions.

Moreover, with regard to tracheotomies, all the guidelines pertaining to breathing tubes apply, with additional concern for the site at the front of the neck. The dressing must be clean and dry at all times. If it looks soiled, somebody did not do his or her job, and you will need to complain about it.

Dialysis

Dialysis is an artificial process that imitates the kidneys. There are two types: (1) peritoneal (abdominal), which requires infusing a special solution into the abdomen and draining it back out, and (2) hemo (blood), which involves the complete transfer of the blood through a machine and back into the body.

Qualified nurses only. Dialysis requires special training because of the complex technology. The consequences of making a mistake can be fatal. Both abdominal and renal dialyses require the understanding of certain scientific principles with the acquisition of technical skills. Nurses must be certified in the type of dialysis they are performing. Most nurses certified in the renal method are also certified in the abdominal. The reverse is not always true. Many floor nurses receive the additional training for abdominal dialysis without learning the hemodialysis process. Hemodialysis requires a higher level of technical skill, so if you or a loved one is scheduled for dialysis, ask the nurse if he or she has a certificate of completion from a dialysis course.

Peritoneal (Abdominal) Dialysis

Peritoneal dialysis is the preferred method if it has to be done on an emergency basis and/or if the need for it is expected to be temporary. The renal specialist (nephrologist) places a dual lumen tube (two tubes in one) into the abdomen. The patient comes out of the operating room with the external end of the tube capped or plugged. The inside of this closed system is sterile. The nurse then hangs a bag of dialysate solution on an IV pole and infuses it into the abdomen. After one to two hours, the nurse drains the solution from the abdomen into a collection bag. While in the abdomen, the solution draws off metabolic waste from the blood (components of urine). The risks of this procedure are abdominal infection, sudden loss of blood pressure with too much fluid draining from the blood (hypovolemic shock), and blood-related complications.

How to reduce the chance of abdominal infection. With abdominal dialysis, infection comes from contamination. It may be unavoidable, but maintaining strict sterile technique in handling the tube substantially reduces the risk. The nurse has to provide dressing changes every eight hours to keep the insertion site as germ-free as possible. Additionally, he or she must treat this tube as a closed sterile system. That means that the crucial moments come every time the nurse opens the system to connect the abdominal tube to the infusion and drainage bags. Thus the nurse must cleanse the tube end with rubbing alcohol or another disinfectant before removing the cap.

In order to minimize the number of times the system is open, nurses will leave the tubing connected after the first dialysis session and simply change the bag each time. This way, the system is reopened only once in twenty-four hours to change the external tubing. You would be helping yourself or your loved one by asking the nurse to tell you what he or she is going to do to minimize the chance of infection. If you are told anything other than what was just described, call the nursing supervisor to observe the procedure.

How to avoid shock. Abdominal dialysis requires a large shift of fluid (two to three liters) into the belly with another shift from the blood vessels into the abdominal cavity. The fluid then shifts back to the outside with the added liquid from the blood. In view of this, there is the possibility of a sudden loss of blood pressure if the exchange takes place too quickly. The inflow and outflow tubes have a thumb-wheel regulator on them by which the nurse can slow down the flow. The blood pressure also must be taken once before, during, and after the procedure. As the patient or family member, you will want to keep an eye on this to make sure it is being done properly.

How to deal with anemia, loss of protein, and loss of electrolytes. The abdominal dialysis process often causes anemia, loss of albumin (blood protein), and loss of electrolytes (potassium, sodium, magnesium, etc.) because the solution also draws off these blood contents. Therefore, it is imperative that the blood be tested every day for low levels of blood cells, albumin, and electrolytes and that replacements are infused as needed. You would avoid serious complications by asking the nurse or doctor to tell you whether these blood levels are normal. If not, the nurse or doctor should make you aware when you or your loved one is receiving replacement infusions.

Hemodialysis

Hemodialysis is the method of choice for those who are in irreversible renal failure. The renal specialist inserts an inner tube into the wrist or elbow in order to join an artery with a vein (arteriovenous, or A-V, fistula). This tube is made of a combination of silicone and plastic (silastic) and can be pierced a few times with a needle without leaking blood. After the nurse inserts the needle into the A-V fistula, the dialysis machine draws all the patient's arterial blood into it for cleansing and then pumps it back into the veins. The blood circulates through the machine, which contains a dialyzer (artificial kidney). The dialyzer has a thin membrane that separates two spaces. Blood passes on one side of the membrane, and dialysis fluid passes on the other. The wastes and excess water pass from the blood through the membrane into the dialysis fluid, which is then discarded. The machine pumps the cleaned blood back to the patient's bloodstream. Although some patients and family members learn to do it themselves without a nurse, in my view the dialysis nurse should remain at the bedside from start to finish. This flow has to be monitored continuously, or there could be dire consequences. The complications commonly associated with hemodialysis are loss of blood volume (with nausea, vomiting, a sudden drop in blood pressure, and shock), blood infection (such as hepatitis, AIDS, and staphylococcus), and worsening of anemia.

How to prevent shock. It is important to understand that when a person is on hemodialysis, all of his or her blood is being pumped into a machine where water is drawn off. This could result in a loss of blood pressure and shock. This is why someone has to monitor the fluid volume loss and replace it as needed. If someone tells you that you or your loved one doesn't need constant monitoring because the machines are more sophisticated, do not accept it. Surveillance is the key to maintaining a proper fluid balance.

How to lower the risk of infection. Hemodialysis has a greater risk of infection than abdominal dialysis. Every machine that you use has had someone else's blood going through it. Additionally, people on dialysis usually have a weakened immune system and are more susceptible to germ invasion. There are two sources of infection: cross-contamination from other patients with infectious disease like hepatitis and AIDS and bacterial and/or viral invasion at the point of needle insertion. There have been many outbreaks of hepatitis among hemodialysis patients reported by the Centers for Disease Control and Prevention. One possible explanation is that the dialysis centers have so many patients that nurses and technicians don't have the time to do a proper disinfection between treatments. You or your loved one have a right to insist on complete disinfection and discarding of all used disposable components before hooking up. If you have any doubts, stop the process, call the supervisor, and complain.

Regarding needle insertion, the silastic tube under the skin, while quite innovative, is not perfect. The nurse has to avoid sticking the needle in the same spot more than once. At some point this becomes less likely, and leaks are liable to occur, causing blood clots to form under the skin. With the patient's immune system in depression, the clot and the leaky tube usually become infected with rapid spread into the bloodstream. The best way to prevent this scenario is for the nurse or technician not to inject the needle into a previous needle mark. Once the needle marks become too numerous to avoid that, it is time for the nephrologist to change the A-V tube. Again, it is up to you to maintain the high standard of quality to which you are entitled. You cannot rely on the system of doctors, nurses, and administrators, because they are simply too busy to be so meticulous.

Dealing with anemia. Anemia is a common complication of renal failure. Patients with chronically high levels of urea in the blood suffer from bone marrow depression, which slows the production of red blood cells. If the dialysis machine is not properly maintained, it can worsen the anemia through blood loss and destruction of red cells in the cleansing process. Thus it is imperative that you check the maintenance record of the dialysis machine before connecting to it. Ask the nurse to tell you what the manufacturer's recommended maintenance schedule is and whether it is being followed.

ICU Psychosis

Another problem associated with critical care units according to the medical literature is what's been called ICU psychosis. In other words, the design of intensive care units actually causes a number of different psychological aberrations, such as psychotic paranoid delusions and hallucinations. Several theories are floating around, but the consensus is that this happens from a combination of the drugs, constant noise, and continuous bright lights. We also see this more often in patients who have had cardiac bypass surgery and those who survived after a cardiac arrest. Besides whatever effect the cardiac interruption seems to have, it is maddening to be stuck in bed, loaded with multiple drugs, exposed to constant bright lights, and surrounded by ventilator noise, electronic beeps, and loud talking nonstop around the clock. Most of my ICU patients have told me they felt like screaming after one day even if they were not psychotic.

The example that most stands out in my mind was a forty-eight-year-old printer I'll call Norman. He was a patient in the coronary care unit at Bellevue Hospital, where I was working about seventeen years ago. One day his heart gave out while I was standing at his bedside. We were all over him in a few seconds, and he survived. His heart stopped three more times, and we were able to revive him. After he stabilized, we took him off the ventilator and removed the tube from his throat. He was making considerable progress, getting stronger every day. The wife and the girlfriend became good friends, with each respecting the visiting rights of the other.

After twenty-five days of normal behavior, Norman started to become combative, and we had to restrain him. Although he still cooperated with me, he would grab my arm or shirt and plead, "Don't let that man get near me!" His face showed stark terror, and he was pointing to Dr. Fox, a world-renowned cardiologist and professor at NYU Medical School. This episode lasted about two weeks until Norman suddenly reverted to his usual self. When I asked him if he remembered anything, he replied, "I believed that I was Superman and that Dr. Fox was Lex Luthor and that he was conspiring to kill me by putting liquid kryptonite in my intravenous line."

"Did you see anything unusual?" I asked.

Norman smiled, hesitated for a moment, and replied, "Dr. Fox was hanging around outside my window."

"Didn't you wonder how he could do that? Your window is on the tenth floor, and there is no ledge or fire escape."

"He was wearing his antigravity belt."

While not all episodes are so colorful, they are disturbing to the patient and family. The best way to deal with this phenomenon, aside from remaining with the patient as much as possible, is to equip the patient with soothing music through a headset. If allowed, familiar items from home might also help, such as framed pictures, favorite souvenirs, keepsake items, religious objects, and so on. Additionally, a portable DVD player with headphones or a laptop computer might offer some pleasant distraction from the surrounding monotony.

Nurses Are the First Responders: They Need Standing Orders

For the balance of this ICU discussion, I speak to the family member because the critically ill patient is usually too sick to give attention to how the staff provides the services. This discussion pertains to those cases where all life-sustaining measures are to be employed for the patient. Families who have requested that the doctor sign a do not resuscitate (DNR) order need not be concerned with first responder emergency procedures.

Standing orders are a set of medical intervention actions that nurses are required to initiate as lifesaving measures before any of the doctors arrive on the unit. You will want the intensive care nurses to be able to perform the following actions in case there is a life-threatening emergency:

1. Start intravenous lines.

2. Initiate cardiopulmonary resuscitation (CPR) (unless there is a DNR order on file).

3. Give certain drugs as appropriate for stimulating heart rate, slowing heart rate, correcting lethal heart rhythms, raising blood pressure, removing excess lung fluid, and correcting blood acidity.

4. Provide intravenous fluid boluses (fast infusion of normal saline) for shock or blood loss.

5. Defibrillate when appropriate (zap the patient with the paddles to correct a lethal rhythm).

As a family member of a critically ill patient who enters the ICU, you should ask to see a copy of the standing orders. If the charge nurse can't or won't show you one, say that you simply want to be certain that there will be an immediate response in case something happens, whether the doctor is in the unit or not. Make it known that you are aware that response time is the most important factor in saving lives. Also, ask the charge nurse to tell you who is responsible for responding to emergencies. Go to those nurses and doctors and tell them how concerned you are about your loved one. Make them promise every day that they will do everything they can. The purpose for asking for this repetitive reassurance is to cause them to think a little more about your loved one's needs.

Where Have All the Nurses Gone?

One of the most important issues for any critical care unit is the staffing. After all, the term *intensive care* means that the care has to be more thorough and rigorous. Each nurse has to spend more time providing for the needs of the critically ill patient. However, there are varying levels of acuity (severity of illness) depending on whether or not the vital signs are stable.

Ideally, no critical care nurse should ever have more than three patients assigned, and the charge nurse should not have any. Sometimes patients cannot survive without one-to-one care twenty-four hours per day. Unfortunately, in most hospitals the reality is that administrators are stretching the nurse dangerously thin with assignments of three to four patients per nurse. This reduces the amount of time and attention that the critically ill patients receive, resulting in catastrophic consequences. The night shifts, weekends, and holidays are the most dangerous times, because it is hardest to find enough nurses for those periods.

In order to assess whether there are enough nurses to take care of your loved one, you will need to know a little about patient acuity, or level of sickness. This way you will be able to ask your assigned nurse, "How many other patients do you have and what are their acuity levels?" This refers to how sick a patient is and how much is going on in the way of tubes and drains. The highest level of acuity is 5. This denotes a patient who has any two or more of the following:

a need for continuously regulating the drip rate of
   intravenous medication to control blood pressure and/or
   heart rate
unstable vital signs
postoperative for open-heart surgery

If any of these conditions apply to your loved one, you have a right to expect a critical care nurse assigned exclusively twenty-four hours a day. If your nurse has even one other patient, this is a dangerous staffing condition, and you should contact your state health department to lodge a complaint. If you don't have Internet access, there is usually a toll-free complaint number that you can get by dialing directory assistance (also toll-free) at 800-555-1212.

To qualify for an acuity level of 4, the patient would have two or more of the following:

> central lines for intravenous fluids and monitoring
> multiple blood transfusions
> open wounds with drains
> endotracheal or tracheostomy tube attached to a
>   respirator
> arterial line for blood pressure monitoring
> Swan-Ganz for infusions and monitoring the heart
>   pumping function

In such a situation, your nurse should only have one other patient to take care of. On the other hand, the charge nurse or supervisor might tell you that your nurse has to take care of two or three others. In that case, you should ask why. In some instances, you will get a reasonable explanation that the acuity of the other patients is low enough to give your family member the attention he or she needs. Most of the time in today's reality, the supervisor will tell you that there are not enough nurses available. At this point, you need to say, "That is unacceptable, and I am going to hold the hospital, the supervisor, and the nurse accountable if anything happens as a result of this dangerous staffing level." Most likely, this will not change anything in that moment, but you will alert the administration to the fact that you are watching how they respond to the situation. As long as management personnel know that you understand the duty that they owe to you and your loved one, they will spend a little more time and energy focusing on patient safety and satisfaction (customer service). When you find yourself in the middle of a critical care staffing shortage, you need to follow up on it every day by stopping at the CEO's office and asking to see him or her. If the receptionist tells you that the CEO is unavailable or not in, you should leave a handwritten or typed note (prepared in advance) in an envelope with the person's name on it. The note, which should be on letterhead that includes your name, address, and telephone number, should read as follows:

Dear Mr./Ms. _____,

    My [husband, wife, parent, sibling, child, etc.] is a patient in your ICU [specify location with bed number]. Her/his name is _____. I stopped by your office on an urgent matter. The nurse staffing in your intensive care unit is at a dangerously low level. My [husband, wife, parent, sibling, child, etc.] is not getting the necessary amount of nursing care because the nurse has to take care of _____ other patients. This is a dangerous situation, and I am worried that there will not be a sufficient response if an emergency should arise. This is unacceptable. As the leader of this institution, you have the authority to make the changes necessary to bring the nursing care up to acceptable standards, and you have command responsibility for the injury or death that will occur if you fail to do so.

    I am so concerned about this situation that I am thinking of contacting the department of health and the local news media. Therefore, I urge you to contact me to tell me what you are going to do to immediately increase the staffing to safer levels.

If you do not receive an answer by the next day, call the health department and the local newspaper editor. Most likely though, you will receive a response from a lower-level hospital executive who will call you to speak on behalf of his or her boss. You will have to judge for yourself whether you are satisfied with the response. In my view, any answer other than "We have increased the staffing levels so that each patient will get the care that he or she needs" requires further action as specified previously. You should also discuss this situation with your doctor and ask about the possibility of transferring to another hospital. Remember that hospital executives are not accustomed to having patients and family members being assertive with a full understanding of what is going on. In this situation knowledge is power.

The Code

Code is the term that hospital staffers use to describe the act of reviving a person who has stopped breathing (respiratory arrest) and/or whose heart has stopped beating (cardiac arrest). Although the basic details regarding cardiac arrest on the regular floors were covered in Chapter 3, I am providing additional information here. The current thinking is that the patient is still alive at this moment because it takes about four to six minutes for the brain to cease its function beyond any hope of waking up. The actual term or phrase used to alert medical, nursing, and respiratory therapy staffers varies from one hospital to another, with *code blue*, *paging Dr. Heart*, *code 99*, and the like being among those used.

For good reasons, the code is one activity that visitors may not observe. First, the person undergoing the code is in a state of near death with a team working feverishly. Your understandable emotional reaction might prevent the staff from focusing on the more important job of saving a life.

Second, there is no way an outsider can evaluate the quality and appropriateness of the procedures and intervene. You have no choice but to trust the code team. There is nothing more you can do until they revive the patient and he or she is stable.

On the other hand, you can take some measures beforehand to assure that your loved one gets the best possible chance for survival. First, you can make certain that the nurses are checking the crash cart at the beginning of every shift to make sure that it has all the necessary drugs and supplies for a code.

Second, you can ask to see if the nurses are testing the defibrillator at the start of each shift to make sure that it is working when needed. The precious minutes lost replacing faulty equipment can make the difference between a person living or dying.

Third, you can find out who has responsibility as the first, second, and third responders to a code. Many hospitals do not have an organized code team approach. The announcement blares out over the intercom, and whoever is available comes running. This is unacceptable. During normal business hours, you will get too many people in the room bumping into each other. On the other hand, at 3 A.M.

you would be lucky to see one doctor. The standards require an organized response with assigned teams who know what to do and where to go. If there is no such plan in effect, you will need to approach the administration and insist that they organize a code response program.

Protecting Yourself or Your Loved Ones in the Intensive Care Unit

- Take a look at the tubes and wires and ask the nurse to explain what each one is and what it is for.
- The intravenous lines have a drip chamber. Look at this to make sure that the fluid is still dripping. If it is not, call the nurse.
- For intravenous lines in the arms, look at the insertion site for any swelling and/or redness. If you see any of this, tell the nurse and continue to follow up until you get action (see "Infusion Lines").
- If the doctor ordered a transfusion of blood or blood by-products (fresh frozen plasma or platelets), do the following (see "Blood Transfusions"):
  - Make sure the nurse matches the serial numbers and the blood type between the transfusion ticket and the label on the blood product unit in the presence of a second nurse. This will help to avoid transfusion reactions from mismatch.
  - To avoid receiving tainted blood (contaminated with the AIDS virus, syphilis, or another infection), tell the nurse and/or doctor that you will not accept blood received from paid donors (such blood must be labeled).
  - For elective surgery, ask your doctor about autotransfusion (removing and storing your blood prior to surgery to be infused if needed).
- If your loved one has a feeding tube, make sure the liquid nutrient is not going in too fast.
  - If there is any complaint of fullness or nausea, get the nurse to turn off the flow immediately.
  - If vomiting occurs, turn the patient's head to one side to prevent choking.
  - If there is any diarrhea, insist on having the feeding discontinued until the problem is resolved.

- If there is a bladder catheter, do the following whenever you visit:
  - Make sure the catheter is not kinked.
  - Make sure the catheter is anchored to the thigh.
  - Check the urine in the bag to see if it is clear yellow. If it is cloudy or blood-tinged, tell the nurse.
- If there is a kidney catheter, take the following precautions each time you visit:
  - Check to make sure it is still attached.
  - Check to make sure it is not kinked.
  - Check the urine bag as for a bladder catheter.
- Keep a careful accounting of how much blood the nurses and doctors are taking out of the central vein or arterial lines. More than 100 cc would be excessive and could lead to severe anemia.
- Throat tubes must be properly maintained to prevent mouth or throat ulcerations as follows:
  - The nurse must deflate the internal balloon every eight hours to prevent pressure ulceration of the vocal cords.
  - The nurse must reposition the tube every two hours to prevent pressure ulcers within the mouth.
  - The connecting tubes must remain clean and dry.
  - The nurse must provide frequent suction and occasional tracheal lavage (squirting about a teaspoon of saline into the breathing tube and applying suction).
- Tips for peritoneal dialysis patients and their loved ones include the following:
  - Check the credentials of the nurse providing dialysis.
  - Make sure the nurses are not contaminating the insertion site.
  - Make certain the nurses keep the system closed as much as possible.
  - Make certain the nurse takes blood for laboratory tests as needed and follows up on the results.
- Tips for hemodialysis patients and their loved ones include the following:
  - Make sure that decontamination procedures are being performed between patients.
  - Make sure the nurse does not inject the connecting needle into any previous needle marks.
  - Ask the nurse to demonstrate that he or she is performing proper maintenance on the dialysis machine.

- To reduce the psychological impact from the intensive care unit, do the following:
  - Stay with the patient as much as possible.
  - Place personal items at the bedside as permitted.
  - Provide miniature entertainment devices, such as a portable DVD player or a laptop computer.
- Pay attention to how many patients your nurse is assigned to. If there are three or more, lodge a complaint with administration, and follow up with the health department if you do not get a satisfactory response.

6

Before, During, and After Surgery: Operating Rooms and Postanesthesia Recovery Units

THE PROCESS OF SURGERY has three components: preoperative (before surgery), intraoperative (during surgery), and postoperative (after surgery). Here, I'll cover the risks at each stage and how to prevent them.

The problem with surgery is that even if everyone does his or her job with full alertness and accuracy, there is still a chance that something could go wrong because there are things going on that make us defenseless. First, the anesthesiologists put us into a state of unconsciousness with drugs, and then the surgeons cut us open and sew us back up with a lot of cutting, manipulation, clamping, and burning in between. Although the providers always intend to control the process to create a beneficial outcome, we are still dealing with a tremendous insult to the human body and mind.

Given the potential complications in all this, we expect flawless performance of every staff member involved so we can get through all the natural hurdles without someone's moment of inattention causing us harm. Watching a surgical team at work is a little like watching professional baseball. Individual skill is not enough. The focus of each team member with good coordination and timing between players determines the outcome. Even the best ballplayers of all time have had days when their game was off. This also happens with surgeons and their team members. Unfortunately, the sad truth in these cases is that the mere absence of perfection can cause disfigurement, disability, or even death.

Additionally, there are many frightening instances where team members simply do not do their jobs. Your best defense against this dilemma is to learn about the most common mishaps that occur in all hospitals. Then you can talk to operating room personnel and administrators ahead of time about what safeguards need to be in play.

One way to accomplish the task is for us to create an imaginary surgical patient. We'll call him Bob Jones. Let's say he has an abdominal hernia. We will follow him through the entire process, taking occasional breaks from the scenario to explain certain situations and give anecdotal illustrations. This learning method may cause some queasiness, but the knowledge you gain could save your life or that of your loved one.

There is an obvious defect in Bob's abdominal muscles, and he needs surgery. There are no alternative treatments. His surgeon has scheduled a hernia repair (herniorrhaphy).

Before the Operation

The first thing that Bob needs is medical clearance. There are no exceptions. An internist has to take a complete medical history, conduct a physical examination, and run a series of tests: an electrocardiogram (EKG), a chest x-ray, a complete blood cell count and chemistry analysis, a blood test for clotting time, and a urine analysis.

If the examining physician leaves out any of these items, Bob could be in trouble. In addition, if Bob has a fever, the doctor must postpone the surgery at least until he identifies the source. This is done because the fever denotes an unknown place of infection that increases the risk of elective surgery to an unacceptable level.

Now Bob is ready to enter the hospital. He goes into a waiting room. A nurse comes out and brings him into her office to offer him

some pre-op teaching. This is a good opportunity for him to mention the common errors covered in this book and ask about the current safety measures. If he does not get a pre-op teacher, he needs to
insist on one because one should never enter the system without first
getting a preoperative conference with a qualified nurse. If anyone
tells Bob that the hospital does not provide preoperative conferences,
he needs to go to the nursing office and ask to speak to the nursing
director. I am certain that at this point the director will provide a
qualified nurse to answer questions.

A Conversation with a Pre-Op Nurse

The nurse may start to focus on what Bob will need to do to enhance
his recovery and minimize complications such as deep breathing and
coughing after surgery. But Bob should turn the conversation around
to first focus on what the staff members will need to do to ensure his
safety. Here is how the dialogue should go:

NURSE: Hello, I am here to provide you with pre-op teaching. Can
    you describe the operation you are going to have?
BOB: Yes. It's a hernia repair.
NURSE: There are a few things you will need to do to give yourself
    the best chance for a successful outcome.
BOB: I would rather talk first about what the staff will need to do
    to give me the best chance for survival.
NURSE: All right. What are your concerns?
BOB: How can I be certain that the staff will not drop me on the
    floor while transferring me from the bed to the stretcher, from
    the stretcher to the operating table, and vice versa?
NURSE: Oh, they won't drop you. They are very careful with
    transferring.
BOB: Are you going to personally guarantee that and be
    accountable if I fall and get hurt during transfer?
NURSE: No, I cannot agree to that. I do not directly supervise the
    doctors and nurses in the operating room.
BOB: Then how can you assure me of safe transfers in your
    hospital?

NURSE: We have strict policies and procedures for safe transfers.

BOB: Good. Would you elaborate on them please?

NURSE: First, transferring from the bed to the stretcher, the transfer person will come to your hospital room with an operating room stretcher. He and your nurse will place the stretcher next to your bed with no space in between, and he will lock all four wheels. Then they will ask you to slide over onto the stretcher.

BOB: Good. Now I know to make sure that they lock the wheels, and I can test the stretcher with my hand before I move. What is the next step?

NURSE: The transporter will bring you to the pre-op holding area, where a nurse will greet you.

BOB: How do I make sure that I don't end up getting one of my kidneys removed instead of getting the hernia repair that I came for?

NURSE: The nurse who greets you will ask you to state your name and then check your identification bracelet and your chart to make sure they all match.

BOB: So if she doesn't do that, I can ask her who she thinks I am?

NURSE: That's a good idea. Correctly identifying the patient is necessary to avoid operating on the wrong person. All surgical patients wear the same gowns and head covers, so even males and females look alike.

BOB: How do I know they will not operate on the wrong side of my abdomen?

NURSE: The procedure and anatomical location of the surgery is supposed to be on the consent form. The circulating nurse has the responsibility to make sure that the surgeon is aware of whom the patient is and that he is aware of the proper location of the initial cut.

BOB: What happens next?

NURSE: The anesthesiologist or nurse anesthetist will come to you and start an intravenous line.

BOB: What if I still have to wait for a long time and I feel scared and nervous?

NURSE: You can ask for some pre-op sedation.

BOB: What happens when the operating room is ready for me?

NURSE: The anesthesiologist or one of his staff will walk you into the room or bring you on the stretcher.

BOB: What about transferring to the table?

NURSE: If you are on a stretcher, they will ask you to slide over after locking the wheels and holding the stretcher against the operating table. If you are walking, you will just sit and then lie down while swinging your legs up. The table height is adjustable.

BOB: How will the surgical team keep me safe during the surgery?

NURSE: The circulating nurse has the duty of keeping you safe in the operating room. She will perform certain routine tasks that will ensure your safety.

BOB: What does she have to guard against?

NURSE: She has to keep track of blood loss, watch for breaks in sterility to avoid infection, make certain that your body is grounded to prevent electrical burns, and make certain that the surgeon doesn't leave any sponges or instruments inside your body.

BOB: Now, what are the things I will need to do to give myself the best chance for a successful outcome?

NURSE: After abdominal surgery, you will experience some pain with deep breathing and coughing, and this may cause you to not want to do it. That will increase the risk of pneumonia.

BOB: What can I do about it?

NURSE: The floor nurses will keep you as pain-free as possible with medications that the doctor orders. They will also give you this incentive spirometer, also known as a lung expander. [The nurse shows Bob a clear plastic device made up of three cylinders with a Ping-Pong ball in each one.] Place the mouthpiece between your lips and inhale through it, causing all three Ping-Pong balls to rise to the top of each cylinder. After doing this for about five minutes, take a deep breath and cough, but first make sure that you have an abdominal binder. That is a wide elastic belt that wraps around your abdomen with a Velcro fastener.

General Anesthesia: The Hidden Risks

This is the transition between the preoperative and intraoperative phases of surgery. I have heard doctors dismiss their patients' concerns by telling them, "You've nothing to worry about from the anesthesia. The risk is negligible—one in ten thousand, or less than one-tenth of 1 percent." This is promoting a false sense of security because the process of putting you under is loaded with danger. One in ten thousand deaths is one too many if you happen to be the "lucky winner." You should also know that most anesthesia-related deaths and incidences of brain damage occur because the anesthetist failed to pump sufficient oxygen into the lungs. This is not the result of some unexplained phenomenon or a full moon. It is the result of an unfortunate mix of sloppy work and arrogance.

Furthermore, the medical community in the United States may have been remiss in failing to explore a viable alternative. During the 1970s there was a great deal of interest in using acupuncture in place of general anesthesia for a number of operations. Though this trend seems to have died out, I wonder if the medical community has arbitrarily denied us the ability to choose an alternative to the risks of general anesthesia. In any case, you should explore the appropriateness of available alternatives, such as spinal or local anesthesia.

Back to our scenario: In a few minutes, the anesthetist is going to render Bob unconscious by injecting some drugs into his veins, putting him into a comatose state. Bob's entire body, including his respiratory muscles, will be paralyzed from an injection of a drug made from curare. This is always necessary to prevent a patient's sudden involuntary movement during surgery, which could cause a slip of the scalpel or another cutting tool.

Bob's life will depend on what happens in the next sixty seconds while the anesthetist secures his airway by sliding a tube into his throat. If the tube goes the wrong way, the respirator will pump the oxygen into Bob's stomach, and his face will turn blue and dark purple. The biggest problem with intubation is that the anesthetist has to do it blindly. He or she uses a laryngoscope to visualize the vocal cords. Then as the anesthetist moves the tube into the throat, it obstructs the view. Thus as soon as the tube is within striking distance, the anesthetist has to complete the forward thrust without visual guidance.

Furthermore, the anesthetist is at a disadvantage in trying to determine the correct tube size. There is no way to measure for the correct diameter. If it is too small, it will leak air and the lungs will receive insufficient oxygen. If it is too large, there is a serious danger of rupturing the trachea and causing a bizarre condition called subcutaneous emphysema. The entire upper body puffs up like a rising soufflé because the negative pressure within the chest literally sucks air into the fatty tissue beneath the skin. This is somewhat rare, but it is well documented and can happen to anyone. The following is how a doctor described such a case that I once reviewed for the patient's attorney: "The endotracheal tube passed through the vocal cords with some difficulty and within ten minutes the patient exploded with tense subcutaneous emphysema throughout his upper body. By tense, I mean beyond anything that I could have imagined. The head, neck, chest, and abdomen were massively edematous to the point that I could not palpate his sternum or his ribs and I was unable to palpate the anterior neck for an accurate tracheotomy." This patient died because once the integrity of the windpipe was violated, it was impossible to establish an airway.

However, this kind of reaction is not necessarily fatal. In other cases, the airway had been established, the air in the tissue dissipated, and the puffiness resolved spontaneously (went away by itself). I witnessed such a case about twenty years ago in the emergency room of Lincoln Hospital in the South Bronx (New York City). An elderly man was brought in by ambulance because he was going into respiratory failure from severe asthma. The intern on duty tried to put a breathing tube that was too large into the man's throat. The trachea ruptured, and I saw the same phenomenon just described. I ran out into the hallway to get help and found one of the senior surgery residents walking along with a cup of coffee. I snatched the cup from his hand and pulled him into the treatment room to show him the patient. The surgeon immediately performed an emergency tracheostomy with the tools that I handed him, and he inserted a breathing tube through it. I was then able to attach it to a respirator. The man survived.

A few days later I visited him in his hospital room. The tracheostomy was closed, the swelling was gone, and he was talking normally. He ultimately went home and returned to his regular activities.

Choosing an Anesthesiologist

When it comes to choosing an anesthetist, we usually accept without question whomever the surgeons recommend. This is because most of us do not understand the process of anesthesia.

Here are a few suggestions to follow before you sign the consent form:

1. Insist on a meeting with the proposed anesthetist.

2. Regard this meeting as though you are interviewing someone for the most important job on the planet (keeping you alive).

3. Ask the applicant to hold out his or her hand, palm down, and rest a piece of paper on it. If the paper is shaking, get someone else to do your case.

4. If the applicant "passes" the paper trick, ask if he or she is a smoker or drinker. If the candidate gets insulted, find someone else.

5. Ask the applicant to describe the intubation process.

6. Ask how the doctor will know that the tube is in your trachea and not in your esophagus. The answer should be that he or she would listen to your lungs and your stomach with a stethoscope to find out where the air is going.

I actually saw a case in which an anesthesiologist fell asleep during a procedure back in 1980 while I was a circulating nurse in the operating room. The seventy-two-year-old anesthesiologist was sitting on his stool, head bowed, sound asleep. I had to wake him up to tell him that the patient was turning purple. Upon waking up to find me operating his ventilator, the anesthesiologist started yelling, "What the hell do you think you're doing?"

I replied, "Your job."

The surgeon interjected, "You should give the kid half your fee."

After the case was over, I overheard the surgeon yelling at the anesthesiologist in the doctor's lounge. Soon thereafter, the other surgeons began refusing to do their cases with that particular anesthesiologist, and he consequently retired. I don't mean to imply that older doctors are always the problem—you just need to be sure that the person handling this tricky procedure is highly skilled and is having an "on" day.

During the Operation

Once the surgeon makes the first cut, there are risks of infection, blood loss, electrical burn from the cauterization device, sponges and instruments being left inside the body, and pressure injuries resulting in skin ulceration and/or paralysis. For this operation, Bob is going to be on his back and completely paralyzed for hours. Since the anesthesia drugs suppress all the person's reflexes, there is also the risk of corneal ulceration, because the eyelids can't blink and the cornea may dry out. Other risks include fluid overload, medication reaction, blood transfusion reaction, and injury during transfer.

It is the circulating nurse's primary responsibility to guard against these occurrences in the following ways:

- Properly ground the patient's body.
- Make certain the nerve plexus areas (armpits and behind the knees) are not pressing against any parts of the operating table or equipment.
- Provide adequate padding to pressurized areas with foam rubber wedges and the like.
- Monitor and report blood loss by keeping track of amounts in suction collection bottles and weighing discarded sponges.
- Monitor sterile technique of surgeons and scrub nurses.
- Measure and record the intake of intravenous fluids.
- Measure urine output and output from any drains.

- Calculate blood loss.
- Count all sponges, instruments, and needles before start of surgery and immediately before final closure.

If you can get a chance to speak to your circulating nurse before you go under, do it. Get him or her to give you the reassurance you deserve. This nurse might just be a bit more diligent knowing that you have a working knowledge of operating room procedure. The circulating nurse is the patient's advocate in the operating room.

I worked as a circulating nurse some years ago in a Chicago hospital. This one case involved major bowel surgery, which necessitated a wide opening of the abdomen. There was profuse bleeding that resulted in the use of 204 gauze sponges. Toward the end of this five-hour case, the surgeon looked up at me and said, "I'm ready to begin abdominal closure. Did you complete the sponge count?"

"We're missing one sponge. I'm doing a recount," I replied.

"Okay, we'll wait."

I recounted the bloody sponges, and the total came to 203. I searched through all the garbage bags, and there was no missing sponge. I looked up at the surgeon and said, "The missing sponge is not out here. Let's do a portable x-ray before you close."

"I am not going to delay closing any further. You keep looking around for the sponge. I'm sure you'll find it on the floor."

"The sponge is likely still inside your patient, Doctor."

"I never leave sponges! Maybe we need to question your ability to count."

"Doctor, this patient is not leaving this room without an x-ray. If we do it now, we save her the added insult of you reopening her and causing more time under anesthesia than is necessary."

"You can take the x-ray after I close because you will not find anything in the patient."

Although the surgeon was violating hospital policy, I could not stop the closure. I notified the supervisor, who in turn called the chief of surgery. By the time he responded, the surgeon had finished closing the skin. In any event, we completed the abdominal x-ray, and the sponge was lying under the large bowel in the lower right quadrant. All surgical sponges have a string woven in that shows up on x-ray. The sponge removal took an additional two hours. No surgeon is perfect, but if this one had been a little less arrogant, his patient would have been better off.

After the Operation: Recovering from the Anesthesia

After the surgical patients survive the worrisome experience called surgery, the first two hours of recovery are also precarious. This is why there is a special unit called the postanesthesia recovery unit (PACU), the former name for which was the recovery room. The first danger is the possibility of trauma during the transfer of the patient from the operating table to the recovery bed. The usual procedure is to have the surgical team grab the sheet that is under the patient and use it to hoist the unconscious patient onto the stretcher at the count of three. Sometimes it is a smooth transition, but often the movement is a jerky one, and the patient comes down on the stretcher with a thud. I have always viewed this practice as cavalier and dangerous. Most internal stitches used to close the nicks in bleeding arteries are made of catgut and can easily snap with movement, resulting in internal bleeding. When this happens, the discovery of it might be too late. The best scenario would still require going back to the operating room to be reopened.

A fifty-three-year-old man I'll call George went in for an arterial bypass in the right leg to counter a blocked artery behind the knee. The lower leg was not getting sufficient circulation and was beginning to turn colors. The operation was successful, George's right lower leg was showing normal color and was warm to touch, and there was a strong pulse in the foot and ankle. The transfer from the table to recovery bed did not go well. The team did not have good support under the affected leg, and they dragged it along and bounced it slightly while they moved him over. The surgeon said, "Hey! Be careful!" He might as well have said, "Don't do that again," because it was after the fact. After that, no one gave the incident another thought.

In the two weeks that followed, George's right leg deteriorated. First, the pulse became diminished and then nonexistent. The foot was cold to touch. The calf muscle swelled up and became hot and hard. This was obviously a blood collection that no one was paying any attention to until one of the nurses complained to the chief of surgery, which caused the vascular surgery residents to come running. They took George back to the operating room and reopened the leg. Apparently, some of the graft sutures had snapped, and the graft was leaking into the calf muscle from the time of the traumatic transfer to the recovery bed. George's leg ultimately developed gangrene, and he underwent amputation. Notwithstanding all the missed opportunities to save the leg, the primary cause was the faulty transfer.

The only way to assure a nontraumatic transfer is to use a transfer device known as a Hoyer lift. The nurses simply place a canvas hammock under the patient before surgery and then attach it to a hydraulic lift. The lift then transfers the patient over to the bed and gently eases him or her down. One or two people can safely accomplish the entire task. It is safer for the patient and prevents staff from injuring themselves in the process. The hydraulic devices are already available in most hospitals. It is a simple matter to change policy to implement its use in the operating room. It is already in use for patients who weigh hundreds of pounds. I advocate its mandatory routine use in the operating rooms of all hospitals for all patients. It might take a couple of minutes longer to complete the transfer, as opposed to four people hurriedly doing one of those "everybody on three" routines, so people will undoubtedly meet this idea with some resistance. Nonetheless, the extra time would be a good investment if it avoids traumatizing a fresh postoperative patient. Although we are not likely to be successful in changing the current standards for transfer, you can request that your surgeon insist on using a Hoyer lift to transfer you from the operating table. If your surgeon agrees to it, he or she has the authority to make it happen.

The first hour in the PACU is the most crucial period. The nurse is required to do a complete assessment with full vital signs every fifteen minutes, followed by half-hour intervals after the first hour. He or she will adjust this interval depending on whether the patient remains stable. This is the place where the nurse must check the patient thoroughly and frequently for any complications from the anesthesia, such as nausea and vomiting.

One of the greatest risks immediately after surgery is choking, because people often vomit as soon as they regain consciousness due to the effects of the drugs. The staff cannot allow patients to heave while lying on their backs, so they must maintain a constant vigil and turn patients on their sides or at least turn their heads to one side at the first sign of vomiting. This is where family members can help. They should become involved in requesting a brief conversation with the PACU nurse to say, "I'm so worried because I hear about the possibility of people choking on their vomit. Please watch carefully so this does not happen."

Many hospitals allow one or two immediate family members to stay with the patient in the PACU at the charge nurse's discretion. If this is true in your case, then it would be a good idea to be there. If any vomiting occurs, the nurse or physician must turn the patient as far as possible to one side. The visitor must not attempt any intervention except for calling out for assistance if there is no staff at the bedside when the vomiting begins.

The other risks of complications are the same as in the ICU.

INSIDER TIPS

How to Protect Yourself or Your Loved One Before, During, and After Surgery

- The preoperative medical clearance must include electrocardiogram (EKG), chest x-ray, complete blood count, complete chemistry analysis, clotting time. Go over this list with your internist (see "Before the Operation").
- If there is a fever, your doctor must first identify the source unless there is a need for emergency surgery.
- Insist on having a session with a pre-op teacher and ask specific questions about the common errors made in the operating room (see "A Conversation with a Pre-Op Nurse").

- Do not blindly accept your surgeon's recommendation for the anesthesiologist. Set up a meeting and ask the anesthesiologist to explain the procedures and the risks (see "Choosing an Anesthesiologist").
- If possible, speak to the circulating nurse and go over the checklist found in this chapter (see "During the Operation").
- Speak to your surgeon about using a Hoyer lift to transfer you or your loved one off the operating table after surgery to reduce the risk of trauma.
- Be with your loved one in the PACU (postanesthesia recovery unit), if permitted, and do the following:
  - Turn the patient's head to one side if any vomiting occurs to prevent choking.
  - If the patient had neck surgery or is recovering from a fractured neck, call the nurse and do not touch your loved one's head.

7

The Mother-Baby Units

HAVING A BABY should be a wonderful, happy experience. And it usually is. But as with any hospital admission, there are risks that you can try to avoid. The hospital birthing process includes four components: prebirth labor, delivery, postpartem baby (care of the infant after birth), and postpartem mother (care of the mother after birth).

The area of the hospital dedicated to childbirth contains the labor and delivery unit, the maternity floor, the well-baby nursery, and neonatal intensive care. This last area requires due consideration because even with the most modern hospitals in the world, tens of thousands of mishaps occur every year during childbirth causing infant death or developmental delays, cerebral palsy, epilepsy, and/or limb deformities. Women giving birth can also suffer complications, usually related to hemorrhaging and/or seizure. Often these complications are due to some kind of abnormality in the birth process. However, some are due to faulty monitoring equipment and a few inattentive nurses and doctors. As well, there are some common calamities related to inappropriate placement of the child during the first day of life that cause death or a lifetime of disability.

Labor

The labor and delivery unit handles the prebirth period and delivery process. This is a time of many anxious and painful hours that seem to last forever. Usually the father and other family members share the anxiety, but the physical pain belongs exclusively to the mom.

Fetal Monitoring

The key activity for the labor period is fetal monitoring. Attaching the mother-to-be to the monitor is usually one of the first actions of the labor and delivery nurse. The purpose of fetal monitoring is early detection of any fetal distress with immediate appropriate action. Fetal distress is due to a loss of umbilical cord blood flow within the uterus, and it is life-threatening to the baby. Action must be taken right away in this case. Even a few minutes lost could be catastrophic.

The nurses have to operate the monitoring equipment correctly, and they must check the readings diligently and frequently. The monitor tracks the baby's heart rate and measures the intensity and frequency of the uterine contractions. The changes in fetal heart rate just before, during, and immediately after the contractions determine whether there is any fetal distress.

The monitor attaches to the mother in one of two ways: externally or internally. The former requires a belt around the abdomen, and the latter necessitates inserting an electrode into the birth canal. Both attach to the same electronic device, with the internal electrode usually producing readings that are more reliable. There is a monitor screen in the birthing room where the mother stays during labor and another one at the nurses' station. The nurse can watch the monitor from either location. Therefore, the nurse does not have to be with the mother constantly during labor, but frequent hands-on assessments are required. The minimum intervals depend on how close the patient is to delivery.

The ongoing observation of the monitor readouts is the nurse's responsibility. The obstetrician or nurse-midwife relies on the nurse to report any signs or suspicions of distress. This is why adequate staffing is of paramount importance. Each hospital has a policy on the minimum number of qualified nurses required to maintain a safe labor and delivery unit depending on the number of beds. Managers and administrators who allow staffing at less than that number are being derelict in their duty.

Another area of concern is the risk of using Pitocin to induce labor, although there are times when the risk of continuing with an overdue pregnancy is considered greater. However, all too often, a few obstetricians order the drug and walk away. Careful monitoring is vital. A sudden increase in the strength and frequency of contractions could result in the passing of meconium (fetal bowel movement in the uterus). This is very dangerous to the baby's lungs because the baby is actually breathing in amniotic fluid, which has the meconium in it. If the meconium reaches the lungs, it can cause pneumonia, and that can sometimes even cause irreversible brain damage. Again, it all comes down to monitoring, which cannot be overemphasized.

A devastating case illustrating the consequences of a monitoring failure is the story of Baby Jane. Her mother, Nellie, was resting in the labor room with the internal fetal monitor. Contractions were intense and seven minutes apart. The monitor screen was visible in the room and at the nurses' station. Nellie was watching the monitor to assure herself that the baby was doing well with its heart rate. The line went flat with the alarm beeping because the electrode had fallen out. She waited a few moments, thinking that the nurse would come running. After ten minutes, Nellie rang the call bell. Everything had been going well up to that point, so she was not panicky—just concerned.

Then the concern turned to frustration when another fifteen minutes passed with no response. Nellie started yelling for the nurse. Still no one responded except for a nurse's aide, who told her that her nurse was busy with other patients and would be in shortly to reconnect the monitor. Meanwhile, Nellie had several big contractions.

It took a total of forty-five minutes for the nurse to come in and reinsert the electrode. The monitor alarm went off immediately, showing a severely slowed heart rate of 65 beats per minute. It should have been around 120. The nurse quickly rolled Nellie into the delivery room for an emergency cesarean section. The baby was blue at the time of birth and survived, but tragically with massive permanent brain damage. No one knew how long the condition existed because the monitor was off for forty-five minutes. Investigation revealed that there were four nurses on duty, and this unit's policy and hospital policy required a minimum of seven.

It is vital that expectant mothers and fathers be aware of the importance of monitoring and understand the dangers of observation failures. While I don't wish to cause any undue apprehension regarding the birthing process during the labor period, asking questions about your concerns regarding the management of the facility is the best remedy for anxiety. The potential consequences of a false sense of security are far worse than being alert and prepared.

The right questions to ask when arriving on the labor and delivery unit are as follows:

- How many nurses are on duty?
- How many nurses are required for safe care?
- What is the normal range for the baby's heart rate?
- How often will you come in to check my condition?
- What will you do if the baby's heart rate is too slow or too fast?

Remember that you have the right to expect the doctor to come and talk to you each time you believe the fetal monitor shows that something might be wrong.

Delivery

In this section, I do not intend to teach principles of obstetrics. My goal here is to offer some ideas for you to gain enough insight to improve your chances of a safe delivery. The cesarean deliveries fall more in the category of operating room procedure, so please see Chapter 6 for those issues. Therefore, here we shall discuss the option of receiving pain control and the use of forceps during vaginal delivery.

First, many women across the United States are now opting for natural childbirth in outpatient birthing centers staffed with nurse-midwives. This movement has gained momentum because of the risk of brain damage, permanent injury, and infant death associated with the use of drugs and forceps. Thus it is advisable, as you seek out prenatal care, to explore the possibility of engaging in natural childbirth with the services of a nurse-midwife. Here are a few safeguards that should be in place for you and your baby's protection:

- Fetal monitoring must be provided during labor.
- There must be an agreement with a covering obstetrician (medical doctor) who will review the prenatal care with the nurse-midwife and provide medical intervention in case of any complications.
- There must be a hospital within a reasonable distance that can receive you and your baby (after delivery) and provide medical care in case of any unforeseen complication.
- There must be a fully equipped crash cart for resuscitation if needed.
- There must be a paramedic ambulance standing by or available within five minutes for transport.

Pain Control

The use of narcotics during the last stages of labor presents some risk to your baby. Narcotic agents like Demerol will depress your baby's nervous system. Although most of the time this does not cause any damage, there is a risk that the drug could make matters worse if the baby has any other problems. For example, if there were any oxygen deprivation because of mechanical pressure on the umbilical cord, a chemically depressed baby would have a more difficult time recovering from that situation. It is important to have an open dialogue with your doctor about such risks and remember that you have the final word.

Another option is spinal anesthesia, also known as an epidural. This involves inserting a long needle into the lower spine and injecting a drug that deadens the lower half of the body. There is less chance that the drug will enter the baby's system because the blood-brain barrier will keep it within the cerebrospinal fluid system for several hours. The problem here is that the anesthetic will weaken the mother's ability to push, and there is a greater likelihood of the obstetrician having to use forceps to pull the baby out.

Forceps and Vacuum Extraction

When you sign the consent form for obstetrical services, you are giving the obstetrician permission to use forceps for extraction if he or she believes that the baby is not advancing quickly enough through the birth canal. The use of forceps causes severe infant head injury in 1 in every 664 births, or 0.1 percent of births. Such injury could result in developmental delays and/or cerebral palsy, a generalized spastic paralysis that comes from permanent brain damage. This brain damage occurs when the traumatic use of the forceps causes bleeding on the brain (subdural hematoma) or brain swelling (cerebral edema) and the condition remains unnoticed and untreated for too long a period. Damage to the eyes such as retinal detachment, which results in blindness, can also occur.

If forceps do have to be used, encourage your doctor to check the baby's head and eyes carefully afterward. You can also inspect your child's head yourself or ask the father or another relative to do it for you. If there is any bruising or indentation on the sides of the head where the forceps grabbed, then you need to ask the obstetrician or the pediatrician to order a CAT scan or an MRI (magnetic resonance imaging) to rule out brain injury or internal bleeding. The child would also need an eye examination to check the retinas. If all you get is assurance that everything is okay, then, depending on your comfort level, you will have to decide whether to accept it or demand a second opinion. However, chances are that if the doctors know that you are concerned about the possibility of damage from the use of forceps, they will carefully scrutinize your baby's condition to rule out internal head injury. The bottom line is that if you have any doubts, you must continue voicing them until you get a satisfactory response.

Additionally, vacuum extraction is available as an alternative to forceps delivery. The obstetrician accomplishes this by placing a suction cup on the baby's head and using a manual or electric pump to increase the negative pressure. Although there is considerable controversy about this procedure in the medical community, the proponents of vacuum delivery claim that it is less traumatic. However, as with any medical procedure or device, there is a set of risks. It boils down to the skill and luck of the person using the device. If the suction is too strong, it is likely to cause scalp trauma, brain hemorrhage, and/or eye hemorrhage. Although there are guidelines as to the safe amounts of negative pressure, a person can cause injury even while remaining within the accepted range. The same advice applies as with forceps deliveries if there is any hint of trauma.

Complications After Birth

The final issue deals with babies who die or suffer severe damage because of events occurring after birth. One type of common error that continues to occur repeatedly is putting a critically ill newborn in the well-baby nursery. This happens for the most part because the pediatrician thought the child was healthy. This is not necessarily negligence unless the infant was blue and barely breathing.

The basis for making the decision on the baby's health is an assessment tool called the Apgar score. This assigns a numerical value of 0, 1, or 2 for each named sign. If all the signs are normal, the baby gets a score of 10. If the signs are absent, the score is 0. A score of 8 or better requires no treatment. The doctor makes this assessment twice: at birth and at five minutes of life.

The table that follows is a sample of the Apgar scoring tool. This assessment tool is the format generally used in hospitals. A score appears for each sign at one minute and five minutes after the birth. If there are problems with the baby, the doctor provides an additional score at ten minutes. A score of 8 to 10 is considered normal, while 4 to 7 might require some resuscitative measures, and a baby with Apgar of 3 or below requires immediate resuscitation.

APGAR Scoring Form for Newborns

Sign	0	1	2	Birth Score	5-Minute Score
A Activity (muscle tone)	Absent	Arms and legs flexed	Active movement		
P Pulse	Absent	Below 100 bpm	Above 100 bpm		
G Grimace (reflex irritability)	No response	Grimace	Sneezes, coughs, pulls away		
A Appearance (skin color)	Blue-gray, pale all over	Normal, except for extremities	Normal over entire body		
R Respiration	Absent	Slow, irregular, feeble cry	Good cry		
Total Score					

The doctors usually base their decision to place the infant in the well-baby nursery on the Apgar score at birth and five minutes after. With an acceptable score, this assessment tool does not enable the physicians to detect any potentially lethal clinical conditions. Additionally, the nurses usually do not transfer the babies until they complete the paperwork and footprints. The child also spends a little time with its mother, so it takes at least thirty minutes to complete the process. If the doctors were required to make at least one additional assessment before sending out the infant, they might detect a problem that was not apparent at birth or at five minutes.

This might have helped in the case of Baby Martha, who had Apgar scores of 8 and 10 at birth and at five minutes of life, respectively. Because of this near perfect score, the pediatric resident placed her in the well-baby nursery. Upon the baby's arrival, the intake nurse noted that her fingers were a little bit on the bluish side. She reported this to the same resident, and he opted to keep the baby in the nursery because the Apgar scores "were so good."

Three hours later the child became severely cyanotic (bluish color due to lack of oxygen) with her heart rate in the high 160s. The resident wrote in his progress note that he decided to continue "observation" and took no action. A few hours later, the baby stopped breathing. There was a rush to bring the infant to the neonatal intensive care and hook her to a ventilator. The unit staff resuscitated the child, but by then it was too late to prevent the severe brain damage that occurred.

Although negligence to that extent is thankfully somewhat unusual in my experience, the problems began with reliance on an assessment tool that is self-limiting. This being the standard of care, one cannot fault the physician for deciding to bring the child to the well-baby nursery. The fault was in the decision to do nothing in the face of the presenting cyanosis. Nonetheless, a change in the standard, with implementation of the Apgar scoring to be repeated three or four additional times for one hour, might help to reduce the incidence of babies being in the well-baby nursery when they should be in neonatal intensive care. If this became a widespread consumer demand, the medical, nursing, and hospital management professions would likely give in.

All new parents whose babies go to the regular nursery should ask, "What assurance can you give me that my child does not need closer observation?"

If the answer is "We last examined your child thirty minutes ago at five minutes of life and it was fine then," that is unacceptable. The answer should be "I'll examine your child again now and I will follow up in an hour to make sure." If that is not the answer you receive, ask the nurse in the nursery to examine your child again to make you feel more comfortable that all is well. Then when they bring the baby to you for the first feeding, carefully check your baby's lips, fingernails, and toenails for any bluishness. Also note the strength of your baby's sucking. If you have even the slightest doubt, insist that the nurse call the attending pediatrician. The doctor then owes you a duty to come and examine your baby—even if it is just for reassurance. This goes back to the underlying theme of this entire book—*never place your total trust in the system.*

Other Childbirth-Specific Issues Related to Hospital Safety

Many people are asking the question, "Is it safer to keep the babies in the rooms with their mothers rather than in the well-baby nursery?" In my opinion it's not. The purpose of having a nursery is to give the mother at least one day to recover from the effects of childbirth. Mothers after delivery are recovering from an exhausting episode with surgery in some cases, and they need rest. The baby is not going to give his or her mother any time off. Thus the well-baby nursery is a better place for the baby at least for the first day of life. It is up to the nursing staff to make it safe. Every hospital providing maternity services must have certain safeguards for the newborns and their mothers against the spread of infection, falls, kidnapping, and bringing home the wrong baby.

Infection Control

The nursing staff of every nursery has to guard against the occasional outbreaks of staphylococcus and other infections. Aseptic technique must be employed to prevent the spread of infection from staff to the babies and from one baby to another. First, staff members are required to wash their hands thoroughly and wear masks and gloves before entering the nursery. They must also discard their gloves, wash their hands again, and put on a new pair of gloves before going from one child to another. Hospital policy is supposed to require that any nurse or nurse's aide who has a cold or any other infectious disease not work in the nursery while they are sick. In addition, the staff must know if a mother had an infectious disease that could have been transmitted during gestation or birth. Infection control issues and isolation techniques are covered in detail in Chapter 9.

Guarding Against Kidnapping

We have all heard of newborns being kidnapped from a hospital. It is a rare occurrence, but it does happen. To avoid worrying about your baby being snatched out of the nursery crib, simply ask the charge nurse to review with you the hospital's policy for providing security. Here is what should be in place:

- The unit should be locked, with video surveillance cameras in the nursery and all exit corridors.
- There should be electronic access locks for authorized personnel only.
- Access should be limited to those staff members who have a reason to be in the maternity unit.
- There should be an alarm system that triggers whenever the doors open without authorized access.
- The doors to the nursery should have electronic locks permitting access only to those who have special identification cards.
- The alarm should cause all security personnel to close all hospital exits and seal off the building until the all-clear signal is given.

Guarding Against Accidental Baby Switching

Identification is the reason for taking the baby's footprint at birth. This hasn't always prevented a baby from going home with someone else's mother, but it has been very effective in ensuring that switching accidents are rare. Additionally, nurses attach a name bracelet and write the baby's family name on a card, which they then place on the basinet. These are all the precautions that the hospital personnel can take to identify your infant. Baby switching occurs mostly during the first few hours, before the mother has a chance to get to know her child very well. There are a few things you can do so you'll be able to tell that you have the right child:

- Inspect your child for birthmarks and/or any other identifying features like dimples, etc.
- Get to know your baby's smile, cry, and scent.
- Check the name bracelet.

- Get a copy of your child's footprint and keep it with you.
- If you have even the slightest doubt, insist on a footprint match.

For a Safer Birth

Labor and Fetal Monitoring

- Before going to the hospital, find out the minimum number of nurses that are supposed to be on duty at any time by asking the nursing office.
- When you first arrive at the hospital and at the beginning of each shift, find out if the number of nurses reporting for work matches the minimum number required. If the unit is short-staffed, ask the charge nurse to assure you that you will get all the attention you need. If you feel that the staffing level is unsafe, contact the hospital management and the health department.
- Make certain that the fetal monitor stays connected and that a nurse is checking it often.
- Ask your doctor to tell you the normal range for the baby's heart rate (number of beats per minute).
- Watch the monitor for the baby's heart rate especially during contractions (this should be the job of the baby's father or birthing coach). If the heart rate falls below or rises above the range set by your doctor (usually 120 to 140) during the contraction, get the nurse, tell her to call the doctor, and don't take "no" for an answer.

Delivery

If you are thinking about using a natural birthing center with a nurse-midwife (some hospitals have them on-site), make sure the following conditions exist:

- Fetal monitoring must be provided during labor.
- There must be an agreement with a covering obstetrician (medical doctor) who will review the prenatal care with the nurse-midwife and provide medical intervention in case of any complications.
- There must be a hospital within a reasonable distance that can receive you and your baby (after delivery) and provide medical care in case of any unforeseen complication.

- There must be a fully equipped crash cart for resuscitation if needed.
- There must be a paramedic ambulance standing by or available within five minutes for transport.

Pain Control

- If you have decided to take a narcotic, be aware that there is a risk of depressing the baby's breathing at birth. Starting with the lowest possible dose would be prudent.
- If you opt for spinal anesthesia or epidural, be aware that it will increase the likelihood that forceps will be necessary.
- After forceps or vacuum extraction delivery, check the baby's head very carefully for any bruising or deformity. If you have any doubts, express your concern and ask for reassurance.

Complications After Birth

- Ask the doctor to examine your baby's color, alertness, and breathing upon arrival in the nursery.
- Check the strength of your baby's suck during the first feeding.
- If you have any doubts, speak up and don't stop until you get a satisfactory response.

8

Zero Tolerance for Bedsores

BEDSORES (ALSO CALLED decubitus ulcers, pressure sores, or pressure ulcers) are the breakdown of skin resulting from excessive pressure that cuts off blood circulation. Friction burns also cause ulcerations when nursing personnel drag their patients on the sheets while pulling them up in bed. This subject deserves its own chapter because bedsores are one of the most common complications of hospitalization and exist in every hospital and nursing home.

According to the U.S. Federal Agency for Health Care Policy and Research (now the Agency for Healthcare Research and Quality), as of 1993, 10 percent of all hospital patients and 25 percent of all nursing home residents develop bedsores during their stay. Empirical data indicate that these percentages are on the rise. Bedsores are usually the result of institutional neglect, and although prevention is difficult, bedsores certainly can be prevented.

Skin ulcers develop from the weight of the body resting on certain areas of the skin for long periods and from unnecessary friction. A primary responsibility of nurses is to relieve that pressure of weight and to avoid the chafing that comes from dragging the patient's buttocks on the sheet. The fact that such a problem persists in every hospital and nursing home tells us that the nursing profession as a whole has not placed a high enough priority on maintaining skin integrity. To that extent, this particular aspect of nursing is an abject failure. Therefore, you will have to learn what duties nurses owe you and your loved ones so you can insist on those services.

My own mother's story illustrates this point and also demonstrates how some interference can really improve the quality of care you receive. My mother, at the age of ninety-one, was living independently. I was visiting her once or twice per week.

One day, about a day before my regular visit, my sister called to tell me that one of Mom's neighbors said she had not seen Mom for three days. Upon learning this, I called the hospital nearest her home and found out that she had had hip surgery because of a fall she'd taken while out walking. Although she gave my name and location to one of the social workers, no one from the hospital called me to tell me that she was there.

The surgery itself was flawless. Unfortunately, within two days after surgery, Mom developed a pressure ulcer on her tailbone (coccyx). Shortly after the doctor transferred her to the rehabilitation floor, the bedsore deteriorated from partial to full-thickness skin erosion (stage I to stage II).

I had asked the nurses repeatedly if she had any skin breakdown. They assured me that she was getting the necessary care and that her skin was fine. They either lied or really did not know about the wound until one of the doctors discovered it. I did not find out about it until the attending physician told me that he had called in a plastic surgeon for a consult to evaluate the bedsore. Even my mother didn't know about the wound until the doctor told her.

Feeling outraged that I had been misinformed, I went to the nursing office and complained to the supervisor. I asked if my mother had been identified as being at risk for bedsores. The supervisor said she would get back to me.

The next day I went back to the nursing office, and the same supervisor told me she had reviewed the chart and that the admitting nurse had identified her as being at risk.

"Was there a plan of prevention?"

"Yes. They were to turn her every two hours, improve her nutritional status, and keep her skin clean and dry."

"Did the nurses implement the plan?"

"To be honest, the documentation leaves something to be desired."

"What's missing?"

"The turning every two hours was not fully documented."

"They left her unattended for several hours at a time, didn't they?"

"I cannot disprove that statement from the record."

"Wouldn't you agree that the presence of a pressure sore speaks for itself?"

"Yes."

"Nevertheless, I am now concerned with the fact that the wound deteriorated to stage II after she arrived in rehab. I want to know what your nurses are going to do about it. When I first asked them if my mother had any skin problems, they lied to me. Now I still cannot get a straight answer from anyone."

"I will ask the rehab nurse-manager to have a conference with you."

A few minutes later, the rehab nurse-manager came and invited me to his office. His first concern was to tell me that my mother had the bedsore when she arrived on his floor, so it wasn't caused there.

I told him that I was not interested in laying blame, but since he brought it up, my mother's wound had gotten worse after she arrived on his floor. He asked me what I wanted, and I told him that I wanted to know their plan for treating my mother's stage II decubitus ulcer. I asked for an air-flotation mattress, instructions to the staff to turn her every two hours while she was in bed, and meticulous wound care. I also asked him to tell me everything else they intended to do to make sure this wound would not get any worse but instead would heal. He assured me that all the things that I requested were happening and were being documented.

The sad commentary is that in a hospital that enjoys a very fine reputation, my mother would have suffered further deterioration if I had not intervened with a complaint. I also fought for her to remain in the hospital when they wanted to send her out with the wound unresolved. As a result of my speaking to the nursing administration, discharge planner, and attending physicians about the liability they incurred allowing my mother to develop a bedsore, Mom remained there for an additional ten days until the wound healed.

However, in fairness to the nursing staff at this hospital, I must point out that once I brought the problem to their attention, the quality of care became exemplary. From this I learned (from the other side of the fence) that if you voice a legitimate complaint, nursing supervisors and staff would likely rise to the occasion and take immediate corrective measures. Conversely, if you say nothing, chances are one in ten in hospitals and one in four in nursing homes that you or your loved one will suffer the consequences of shameful negligence.

Bedsores may not sound serious, but the loss of skin integrity with even a slight break puts the patient on a slippery slope toward a painful course of deterioration and infection. The skin is a complex organ. One of its primary functions is to shield the rest of the body from a hostile outside world. Bacteria and viruses swarm all over its surface like an army of invaders looking for a breach in the defensive barriers. Once even the slightest breach occurs, the enemy invades and destroys without mercy. In such cases, the nurses, charged with preventing the breakdown, are like sentries who fall asleep at their posts.

The protective barrier function of the skin also works the other way. Thus an ulcer as well results in the loss of body fluids containing precious blood cells, protein, and minerals. The same breach that allows the enemy to invade causes the defending army to lose its weapons and ammunition. For that reason, the slightest skin break can be devastating to one for whom the stress of illness or injury has already strained the immune system.

The principle that I am clarifying here goes to the standard legal definition of the scope of practice of a registered professional nurse that you will find in every state and U.S. territory. "A registered professional nurse diagnoses and treats human responses to existing and potential health problems through such actions and interventions as health counseling, health teaching and actions restorative to life and well-being. . . ." (New York Education Law, Section 169; the balance of this statute refers to administering physician-prescribed regimens and the prohibition against altering any existing course of medical treatment.)

Accordingly, the responsibility of diagnosing the potential for pressure ulcers and providing preventive measures and daily follow-up falls exclusively on the registered nurses. First, the admitting nurse must initially assess whether you or your loved one has any risk factors that predispose to pressure ulcers.

Second, the nurses must devise a nursing care plan detailing what preventive action they and their subordinate staff (licensed practical nurses and nurse's aides) must take. If you find out there is a likelihood of forming pressure sores, you have a right to demand that the nurse show you or tell you what the plan is. Once you learn the one method of prevention that works, you will be able to assess whether the nursing care plan is adequate. Anything less is not acceptable because the appearance of even a small bedsore results in a high risk of infection.

Finally, the nurses must follow up daily and document the results of the protective measures. It only takes an hour for the skin to start breaking down. Therefore, early detection of prolonged pressure is paramount.

Who Is at Risk for Bedsores?

In making the assessment, your admitting nurse must determine whether any one or more of the following risk factors exist:

age over 60
spinal cord paralysis
stroke
nervous system disease
poor circulation
diabetes
confined to bed

altered level of consciousness
confusion
bladder incontinence
bowel incontinence
diarrhea
anemia
dehydration
malnutrition
obesity
emaciation
reduced mobility (traction or body cast)

The usual procedure is to assign a value of 1 to each risk factor and add up those that exist. The totals then translate to one of the three levels of risk as follows: 0 to 6 indicates low risk, 7 to 13 indicates moderate risk, 14 to 18 indicates high risk.

The parts of the body that are susceptible to pressure ulcers are the heels, ankles, knees, buttocks, tailbone, lower spine, shoulder blades, ears, and back of the head.

Why Bedsores Occur

Bedsores most often develop when continuous pressure closes off the microscopic blood vessels (capillaries) that deliver oxygen and nutrients to the skin cells. The surface skin cells in the affected area experience a buildup of metabolic waste and then die. Once a cell dies, it bursts and the fluid causes swelling in the surrounding area. This makes the blood circulation even worse. It takes as little as one hour from the start of pressure until the initial signs of skin damage appear. The nurse must relieve the pressure at no more than two-hour intervals by turning the patient and providing meticulous skin care. The skin care consists of keeping the pressure points clean and dry and massaging those areas at least once every eight hours. Washing and drying reduce the amount of surface bacteria, and massaging increases the blood circulation. The failure to provide these basic nursing services is the underlying cause of all bedsores. Since hospital nurses neglect tasks 10 percent of the time, you as the patient or family member have to pay attention and speak up if these tasks aren't being done and documented. It is difficult to understand why the need to maintain skin integrity is being neglected on such a large scale. While there is no legitimate excuse, one possible explanation is that most hospital staff nurses are overworked and in a perpetual state of exhaustion. While each nurse is accountable for individual negligence, we need to examine the culpability of hospital executives who fail to provide the fiscal management necessary to generate reasonable working conditions and maintain adequate staffing.

Skin ulcerations also occur because of friction caused by dragging the patient's buttocks on the sheet. This happens because nursing personnel pull their patients up in bed by their arms rather than using a drawsheet (a small-sized bedsheet that nurses use like a sling to move the patient in the bed). This may be a common practice, but it is, nonetheless, bad for the patient and, so, is unacceptable.

If you or your loved one is entering the hospital with any of the risk factors listed earlier, tell the admitting nurse that you want to be sure that no bedsores develop and you will be watching and hold nursing staff and the hospital accountable if there is any skin breakdown. You need to be resolute and firm because the effect of bedsores is usually quite damaging. The same negligence that caused the wounds to develop will likely allow them to worsen. The case history that follows is not pretty, but it's important for you to realize that bedsores are not trivial and it's critical that you be vigilant.

Dorothy was a thirty-nine-year-old mother of four. She had diabetes and she was obese, weighing about three hundred pounds. The physician in the Medicaid clinic that she attended admitted her to the hospital because she had a wound that wasn't healing on the inner aspect of her left thigh. Two weeks earlier, Dorothy had outpatient surgery at the clinic to remove a cyst. The wound became infected while Dorothy was having her usual problem of keeping her blood sugar under control because of the nature of her diabetic condition. High blood sugar causes infections to become worse and also slows the healing process.

After three weeks in the hospital, Dorothy spiked a fever at 103°F. She became lethargic. The blood culture showed that she was septic (had bacteria in the blood), and a culture of her wound showed the same bacteria. The sensitivity tests showed that this bug was resistant to most of the available antibiotics. The course of treatment was long and arduous—it took three months. During this time, Dorothy was delirious and bedridden. She became incontinent of feces (meaning that she was unable to control her bowel movements). She had enough risk factors to classify her as a high risk for bedsores.

Dorothy's sister and children visited her every day. The sister and her eldest child, her eighteen-year-old son, knew that she was not getting adequate nursing care and started taking photographs. They always found her lying flat on her back with excrement in her bed. When Dorothy had a bowel movement, the nursing staff would usually let her lie in it for about four hours before cleaning her up. Her family complained to the nurses on the floor and got little or no response.

As you may have guessed, Dorothy developed a wound, which started as an area of redness, turned white, and then started to break down. First, there was fatty tissue exposed with weeping of clear fluid. Then infection set in. Next, the deterioration continued until the muscle was showing through. There was dead tissue with copious amounts of coffee-colored pus draining. Finally, there was exposed bone with osteomyelitis (infection of the bone).

Although the thigh wound healed, Dorothy died of overwhelming infection from the pressure ulcer. Her sister and eldest child might have been able to save Dorothy's life if they had known how to assert themselves with the hospital hierarchy and even the department of health, if necessary. There were many opportunities to stop the worsening of her condition during the first two months of hospitalization. What Dorothy needed was scrupulous basic nursing care.

How Bedsores Can Be Prevented

Time and attention are the basic ingredients for preventing bedsores. Both are becoming scarcer with the ever-dwindling number of nurses in the workforce. When a person is bedridden, the main thing to do for prevention is to reposition the patient from side to back to the other side every two hours. There are no exceptions, and there should be zero tolerance for failure. The hospital must supply forms for the nurses to document the length of time that the client spends in each position. There are varieties of designs, but I shall give you one for illustration here.

Turning and Positioning Record

Date: 11/20/02
Shift: 7–3

Position	Left Lateral	Supine	Right Lateral	Supine
Start Time	0700	0900	1100	1300
End Time	0900	1100	1300	1500
Length of Time	2 hrs.	2 hrs.	2 hrs.	2 hrs.

Date: 11/20/02
Shift: 3–11

Position	Left Lateral	Supine	Right Lateral	Supine
Start Time	1500	1700	1900	2100
End Time	1700	1900	2100	2300
Length of Time	2 hrs.	2 hrs.	2 hrs.	2 hrs.

Date: 11/20–21/02
Shift: 11–7

Position	Left Lateral	Supine	Right Lateral	Supine
Start Time	2300	0100	0300	0500
End Time	0100	0300	0500	0700
Length of Time	2 hrs.	2 hrs.	2 hrs.	2 hrs.

The hospital should supply the following devices to protect the skin of a person at risk: foam rubber heel pads, sheepskin bed pads, an air or water mattress, an air-flotation bed, a drawsheet, and Chux.

If the hospital has not supplied any of these, ask for them. Keep at it until everything has been supplied. Don't take "no" for an answer and don't assume "yes" means it will happen. Follow up to be sure.

The idea behind all of these devices is to relieve pressure by redistributing it. If there is compression of any single body part for too long, the skin will break down and an ulcer will develop. There are no exceptions. There is a simple care plan that should be in place in every hospital for every patient who is at any level of risk of developing pressure ulcers.

The care plan on the facing page is what you should be looking for. Accept nothing less. Let the executives know that any skin breakdown would be a disgrace and that you will take legal action if there is any breach of duty. There is no valid excuse for not following every aspect of this prevention protocol. Any hospital executive who claims this is too much to expect because of the nursing shortage is guilty of false advertising when the hospital is held out to be a facility that delivers quality care in accordance with accepted standards, because the standard is *zero tolerance for bedsores*!

What to Do When Prevention Fails

All right, let us say you discover that your loved one has a bedsore, as I discovered when I visited my mother. Although this problem should be nonexistent, as long as substandard care is rampant, there will be pressure ulcers. This is an unpleasant fact, and we have to deal with it by going to the second line of defense—healing the wounds at an early stage.

The first priority is to make sure that everyone knows about it— the charge nurse, nursing supervisor, director of nursing, attending physician, social worker, chief of medicine, risk manager, patient's advocate, and CEO. They might think that you are overreacting, but you will get the message across that you will not tolerate anything less than an aggressive approach to this potentially lethal problem. If you do not act as if this is life or death, neither will they. Addi-

Nursing Care Plan

Nursing Diagnosis	Nursing Orders (Interventions)	Goal
High risk for decubitus ulcers due to poor mobility and emaciation	• Turn patient every two hours.	*No bedsores*
	• Keep skin clean and dry.	
	• Immediately remove excrement and clean the skin with antibacterial soap in case of incontinence.	
	• Provide routine skin care and massage bony areas every eight hours or more often as needed.	
	• Place heel pads.	
	• Place sheepskin under buttocks.	
	• Place drawsheet.	
	• Use drawsheet to move patient up in bed.	
	• Never allow any part of skin to drag on the sheet.	
	• Obtain antipressure mattress.	
	• Provide fluids for adequate hydration.	
	• Provide nutritional counseling and supplements for adequate nutrition.	

tionally, find out if there is a functioning pressure-ulcer prevention committee (all hospitals are required to have one, but for some it is in name only). If there is, go to the chairperson and say that you will forgive their failure if they can show you an aggressive care and treatment plan.

There are many differing opinions on how to treat wounds. The big pharmaceutical companies have a variety of high-technology dressings. The bottom line is that the human body has to heal itself.

There are products that will aid the process, but that is a subject for another book. You will have to consult the attending physician and see which he or she prefers. Whatever the doctor prescribes, the regimen must provide the following protocols:

- Clean the wound with irrigation and surgically remove all necrotic (dead) tissue one time only.
- Increase blood flow to the affected area.
- Absorb drainage away from the center of the wound while keeping it moist. Do not let it dry out.
- Avoid any pressure on the wound area.
- Do not disturb the wound in any manner. The initial healing stage is very delicate.
- Test the blood for the patient's nutritional status and improve it if needed.
- Test the blood for anemia and correct it if needed.
- If diabetes is present, check the blood sugar every eight hours and keep the blood glucose levels between 90 and 180.

You have the right and responsibility to demand that the physician assure you that the list of orders will accomplish all the preceding items. If you are unable to get that assertion, then find another doctor—preferably someone who knows how to promote healing of chronic wounds.

Clean Surgically Once Only

First, the surgeon should only get one shot at cleaning the wound. I once had an eighty-eight-year-old male client who had a gaping wound on the inner side of his right foot. He was going to a podiatrist once every week. Every time I inspected the wound during the dressing change, it was squeaky clean. The problem is that there was no progress in healing. I found out that the podiatrist was scraping the wound bed every week. By doing this, he unwittingly removed all the material that the body produces for healing (granulation). This was like planting seeds in a garden, then pulling out all the seedlings by the roots and wondering why nothing grows. When I explained to the podiatrist what was happening, he stopped the weekly meddling, and the wound started to heal.

New Ways to Increase Blood Flow

Most doctors will tell you that increasing blood flow to the wounded area is not realistic. That is because they are unfamiliar with a new technology called pulsed high-frequency high-peak power electromagnetic energy. One machine, the Diapulse® Wound Treatment System™, produces bursts of energy (up to six hundred per second) sufficient to do the job. Its manufacturer is the Diapulse Corporation of America. This safe, heatless device increases blood flow and reduces swelling. Dozens of studies published in major medical journals have demonstrated total success in healing chronic wounds with Diapulse by increasing blood flow and reducing edema (swelling). I have used this machine on hundreds of chronic pressure ulcers in nursing homes, hospitals, and private dwellings with complete healing in all cases. Some of those wounds were open to the bone with gangrene and infection and had been around for more than a year. The only problem with this gadget is its obscurity. Few doctors or nurses know about it, so it remains in the realm of alternative medicine. However, it is accessible if you can convince your doctor to order it. It is not cheap to use, but some health plans may cover the cost under medical equipment rentals. There is no risk in using it, and it could make a difference between healing or overwhelming infection and death. You can get full information from the website diapulse.com and share with the physician or nursing staff.

Drainage

Every wound that is on its way to healing will produce a lot of drainage. It is important to draw the fluid away from the wound without touching it. That means no patting or wiping. A product called OpSite® forms a clear plastic barrier over the wound. The manufacturer engineered this film to allow fluid to flow through one way only. This allows absorption with gauze with no backflow, thus reducing the incidence of infection. The downside is that nurses often leave this dressing on too long, and it loses its effectiveness. This causes pooling of fluid and can lead to infection. The usual and customary practice is to leave the OpSite in place for three days while changing the outer gauze layer every eight hours. If the staff members want more information about this product, you can direct them to opsite.com.

Another way of drawing off fluids while maintaining a proper wound environment is using moist gauze covered by a dry layer. This could be a problem if the dressing dries out because the gauze sticks to the wound, and the nurse in pulling it off rips out all the healing factors. To avoid drying, hydrogel is very useful. This water-based gel helps to maintain a moist environment. There are several brands to choose from, and it is important that the nurse selects one that will not liquefy at body temperature. Otherwise, it would be the same as using water, which leads to drying.

Avoiding Pressure

Avoiding pressure goes back to the need for vigilance in turning the person every two hours and providing pads and a flotation mattress. No treatment will be effective if the compression continues unabated. This is why if you have discovered a bedsore, you have to make time to visit the administrative people and take them to task. Do not simply talk to the nurse. I cannot overemphasize that this is a matter of life or death and you must get people to pay attention. Every hospital has some good people who are genuinely concerned about patients or at least who are concerned about maintaining a good public image. On the other hand, if you cannot get anyone to respond, call the state health department and file a complaint. Again, your goal here is to simply get the nurses to turn the patient every two hours, document the turning so you can check it, and provide padding and a flotation mattress. They must stop the prolonged pressure.

Let the Wound Heal

It is bizarre that few doctors and nurses really know how to treat a wound. Most of them live by the clean-and-scrub principle. They clean and scrub the wound every time they change the dressing so there is nice clean-looking pink tissue. However, that wound will never heal because the initial stages of healing are at the cellular level, with healing tissue cells literally floating across the "lake" to implant themselves throughout the wound. This early stage of healing is very delicate. Any outside interference such as dabbing, touching, wiping, or irrigating will remove the granulation cells and retard or stop the entire healing process. Only people with adequate education and training in wound care should change the dressing. There is a nursing specialty called ET (enterostomal therapy). These are the wound care experts. They started as specialists in caring for patients with colostomies and are now involved in all wound care. You should insist that the hospital provide an ET nurse to consult with the staff on how to best handle the pressure ulcer that you are dealing with.

The Importance of Nutrition

Nutrition is crucial to healing. The blood albumin levels will give the physician a clue as to whether the patient has enough protein to effect healing. Food protein is the basic building block for manufacturing new cells, and that is precisely what is needed for healing.

As with everything else, you will have to chase down the nurse and physician to discuss the patient's nutritional status. When I first found my mother in the hospital, I repeatedly asked, "What is her nutritional status?" When they told me that her albumin was low, they told me that the nutritionist set up a plan to give her liquid protein supplements. There were several cans of Sustacal® sitting at the bedside, unopened like decorations. When I asked Mom why she was not drinking it, she said, "It tastes like crap!" Most people would probably agree with her. Nevertheless, I coaxed her to drink it, and she did once she understood why it was so important to her well-being.

Unfortunately, I could not rely on the hospital staff to encourage her to increase her intake. Realizing that Mom needed more incentive to eat, I brought her favorite healthy foods from outside. That is when she started to substantially increase her food intake. Her nutritional status improved within a few days, and this played a crucial role in her healing. Remember that aside from being unable to count on the hospital personnel to fully explain the importance of nutrition, you cannot rely on hospital food, because it usually is unappetizing, is unappealing, and tastes terrible. Make the effort to have food brought in if at all possible.

Anemia

You will need to find out if you or your loved one is anemic. The people who are at risk of getting bedsores are sick, thin, and frail, and many of them have just had surgery. Chances are that many of them will have some level of anemia. Anemia is a chronic condition of having too few red blood cells. The red blood cells are the vehicles by which oxygen and nutrients get to all the cells in the body. The injured area cannot heal without these basic ingredients.

If the doctor tells you that there is anemia, you need to ask what is going to be done about it. There are several different types of anemia. Medical science identifies two of them as to cause: iron deficiency and blood loss. In both of these cases, the solution is not complicated. For iron deficiency, iron supplements should be helpful, and for blood loss, the usual treatment is infusion of packed red blood cells (concentrated blood). See Chapter 5 for information on blood transfusions.

Bedsores and Diabetes

When the pressure-ulcer victim is diabetic, the high blood sugar levels accelerate the process of infection and gangrene. Wounds tend not to heal, and bacteria thrive on the added sugar. It's crucial that the physicians and nurses work with the patient to keep the blood glucose level between 90 and 180. Some clinicians will advocate a slightly wider or narrower range, which is also acceptable. Keeping the blood sugar within normal limits will reduce the probability of infection.

Zero Tolerance for Bedsores

There must be zero tolerance for bedsores. The accepted standard is to evaluate every patient every day as to the risk of developing pressure ulcers and to perform all preventive measures required for patients in jeopardy of losing their skin integrity. As a nurse, I find it difficult to admit that the nursing profession has failed in its duty to protect its hospital and nursing home clients from skin breakdown. It would be much easier to say that bedsores are not always preventable. However, unless the patient records can demonstrate that the ulcer occurred despite carrying out all reasonable preventive measures, institutionalized negligence remains the root cause of the epidemic. Don't let that happen to anyone you care about.

INSIDER TIPS
_____

Preventing Bedsores

Make certain the nurses provide care as follows (see "How Bedsores Can Be Prevented"):

- Turn patient every two hours.
- Keep skin clean and dry.
- Immediately remove excrement and clean the skin with antibacterial soap in case of incontinence.
- Provide routine skin care and massage bony areas every eight hours and more often as needed.
- Place heel pads.
- Place sheepskin under buttocks.

- Place drawsheet.
- Use drawsheet to move patient up in bed.
- Never allow any part of skin to drag on the sheet.
- Obtain antipressure mattress.

Treating Bedsores

Make certain that the nurses are providing care as follows (see "What to Do When Prevention Fails"):

- Clean the wound with irrigation and surgically remove all necrotic (dead) tissue one time only.
- Increase blood flow to the affected area.
- Absorb drainage away from the center of the wound while keeping it moist. Do not let it dry out.
- Avoid any pressure on the wound area.
- Do not disturb the wound in any manner. The initial healing stage is very delicate.
- Test the blood for the patient's nutritional status and improve it if needed.
- Test the blood for anemia and correct it if needed.
- If diabetes is present, check the blood sugar every eight hours and keep the blood glucose levels between 90 and 180.

9

Hospital-Acquired Infections

ACCORDING TO A Centers for Disease Control survey published in 1992, more than two million people annually pick up infections in the hospital, with approximately ninety thousand deaths caused by these infections. Hospital-acquired contagions account for about one-half of all hospital complications. Therefore, we are dealing with a problem on a massive scale.

There are two basic pieces to learning the cause and control of this dilemma: (1) It is the nature of the beast—infected people go to hospitals because that is where they need to be. (2) Human behavior plays the largest role in the spread of infectious organisms.

To begin with, from a public health perspective, every hospital is a micro-bug magnet. Sick people go to hospitals, and that includes everyone who has a contagious disease. So a hospital is where you will find a concentration of people with tuberculosis, hepatitis, anthrax, influenza, AIDS, herpes, syphilis, gonorrhea, pneumonia, viral meningitis, and every other conceivable infection. The goal of the nurse-epidemiologist is to prevent the spread of communicable diseases within the hospital.

Regarding human behavior, there are at least eleven ways in which hospital personnel contribute to the incidence of infection:

- failure to wash hands between patients
- failure to change gloves between patients
- failure to provide ventilator maintenance
- failure to provide catheter care
- contamination in the operating room during surgery
- breach of sterile technique during dressing changes
- breach of sterile technique during insertion and maintenance of vein catheters
- failure to properly dispose of biohazard waste
- failure to isolate patients with infectious diseases
- breach of isolation technique
- failure to provide appropriate treatment for infection

Cleanliness First

Humans are natural vectors. A vector is an organism that carries disease-causing microorganisms from one person to another or from a contaminated area to a clean area or noninfected person. In that context, health-care personnel who, out of carelessness, fail to take reasonable precautions are behaving like mosquitoes and flies.

Therefore, the standard approach to curtailing the spread of infection must focus on the behavior of health-care professionals and allied staff. In fact, reducing the contagion in hospitals is so dependent on human behavior that most states require all hospitals to include infection control in their employee orientation and continuing education programs. Moreover, every hospital must have an infection control plan in order to qualify for JCAHO accreditation and to conform to public health codes. What is missing with all of this fanfare is that no one has bothered to let you in on the deal. I have not heard of an infection control class for patients and their family members.

You see, no supervisor can follow staff members around to make sure they wash their hands after each patient contact. So it's a very good idea for you to enforce the hospital policy by telling the nurse, doctor, or therapist, "I didn't see you wash your hands. For my peace of mind, would you mind doing it at the sink here in my room?" If you get any response other than total compliance, reply with, "I am sorry, because of the high rate of hospital-acquired infections, I cannot let you touch me [or my child, if in a mother-baby or pediatric unit] unless I see you wash your hands or apply antibacterial gel and put on a new pair gloves." If you don't get the desired response, your next comment should be, "I would like to speak with your supervisor about your refusal to wash your hands prior to patient contact."

New Gloves for Each Patient

Another undesirable behavior is someone who enters your room still wearing the gloves used on the last patient. This is blatantly reckless, and you would help yourself and others by speaking out against this. On the other hand, it is possible that the person put on a new pair of gloves just prior to entering your room and you did not see it. In that case, you should always ask if those gloves are new. If you have any doubts, you should insist on them being changed anyway. Protecting your health is more important than shielding the staff person's ego, although any request can be made in a way that does not arouse anger and resentment (see Chapter 11 for details on communication).

Ventilator Maintenance

The breathing tubes are prone to harboring infectious bacteria. If you have seen a staff member come into the room, disconnect the plastic accordion tube, shake the water out, and reconnect it—that is the respiratory therapist. This apparatus needs to be changed at regular intervals, every one to three days. Hospitals with cash-flow problems are likely to require changing these disposable items less often to save money. While there is some leeway in this, the respiratory therapists and nurses must keep these tubes clean and dry at all times. The best way to accomplish this is to have two sets for each bedside so the respiratory therapy department can clean one while the other is in use. Additionally, the therapists and nurses must be diligent in removing the water that collects in the external airflow system. The moisture transforms the system into a breeding ground for infection. The respiratory therapists are required to keep a record of their visits and what they do. If you have any doubts as to whether the respiratory therapists are maintaining the respirator system properly, you can ask the nursing supervisor to check the records. Most hospitals have a policy to prohibit patients and their designees from reading their hospital charts.

Caring for Bladder Catheters

Many people have to have catheters inserted to drain urine from the bladder. The usual rationales for this are to bypass urinary blockage, to satisfy the need for precise measurement of urinary output, and to protect skin integrity from bladder incontinence. The presence of a catheter removes the natural defense against bladder infection because the rubber tube provides an open road for invading microorganisms. Consequently, the longer the catheter remains, the greater the risk of infection. Each day that you or your loved one has a bladder catheter remaining, you should ask the physician to justify keeping it there and inquire as to what would be the consequences of removing it now. Additionally, if the catheter must remain, the standards of care require that the nurses provide catheter care every eight hours. This involves cleaning the tube with antiseptic solution starting at the urinary opening and wiping away from the body. The nurses then follow the cleaning with application of antibiotic ointment (usually ointment with iodine) at the point of entry. It is best to include this procedure in a checklist that you would go over with the head nurse every day to make sure that the staff members are performing all the required tasks.

Operating Room Contamination

A major source of sometimes-lethal infection is contamination in the operating room during surgery. If you are undergoing surgery or sitting in the waiting room waiting for a loved one, there is nothing you can do to observe for potential mistakes. Moreover, when you sign the consent form, you agree with the statement that you accept the possibility of infection as being a reasonable risk.

Nonetheless, there is a standard of behavior for minimizing the incidence of contamination, called sterile technique. The one person in charge of watching the rest of the team for contamination is the circulating nurse. In addition, conscientious surgeons and technicians will watch each other and call out when a breach of sterility occurs. The person who committed the breach will change gloves and sometimes even regown when there is a doubt. This is not a perfect system, but it is all we have. The only way that you can have a positive influence on minimizing your chances of intraoperative infection is to have a discussion with your surgeon about sterile technique and, if possible, arrange a meeting before surgery with the circulating nurse. You will increase your comfort level if you can ask for and go over a list of routine operating room precautions for reducing the risk of contamination.

Furthermore, there is a group of air-filtration devices called laminar airflow. With these systems, sets of fans keep the air moving in one direction through microfilters, which results in removing a significant amount of germs from the air in the room. If your preferred surgeon can give you a choice of hospitals, find out which one has such air-cleaning mechanisms. Operating rooms built or renovated within the last ten years are more likely to have effective germ-reducing air-filtration technology.

Dressing Changes

Although the handling of surgical wounds or burns determines the risk of infection, the presence of such a problem does not prove that there was a breach in sterile technique. There is no such thing as complete sterility in open air, and the hospital bed is a "dirty" environment. Nonetheless, there is a basic method for changing a "sterile" dressing to minimize the risk of wound infection. In the process of removing the old dressing and then opening the new gauze pads and other materials and applying them, the wound and the dressing materials must not touch bare hands or any nonsterile item in the patient's surroundings. Thus persons providing wound care first spread out a sterile sheet of absorbent paper with plastic backing. Then they open the dressing pack and dump it onto the sterile field without touching the contents. Following that, they don a pair of sterile latex or vinyl gloves, treat, and dress the wound. The important principle in this procedure is to identify sterile versus nonsterile and keep the two worlds separated.

Vein Catheter Sterility

Indwelling intravenous catheters are another major problem in dealing with hospital-acquired infections. This includes peripheral and central intravenous lines. Once the nurses or doctors place these objects into the arm or chest, they attach a fluid-filled plastic bag to the catheter with a long tube and a connector at the insertion site. The inside of these tubes must remain sterile because we use them to inject fluids directly into the bloodstream. The danger is that nurses have to open these systems at regular intervals to add medication and replace the empty fluid bags. The initial setup also carries with it a risk of infection. The intravenous tubing has a cap on the connecting end that the nurse or doctor has to remove just before attaching the line to the vein catheter. He or she has to do this quickly because there is blood pouring out of the opened vein. If this person pulls off the cap with his or her teeth, you must consider the intravenous tube to be contaminated. In that case, you will have to stop the procedure and ask for a restart.

Several years ago, I went to a community hospital emergency room with a case of food poisoning. The doctor decided that I should have an IV, so one of the nurses came over to start it. She inserted the short catheter into a vein in my right wrist. Then she pulled the cap off the tubing with her teeth. I immediately told her that she could not connect that tube to my vein. She insisted that it was fine because her mouth only touched the cap. I didn't back down, and eventually, after giving me some dirty looks, the nurse got a fresh tube and opened it properly.

Although this was an unpleasant encounter, this woman was actually a competent professional. She was using a shortcut that reduced the length of time required for that job. It made her more efficient with regard to the number of tasks she could perform in a given time period. It is quite common for nurses to learn such shortcuts from each other. Consequently, some of them develop sloppy work habits (from an infection control perspective) and unwittingly cause catastrophic outcomes. These kinds of incidents happen very fast, and usually no one notices. That is why you, the hospital user, have to be ever diligent in watching the people providing the services. Most of the time, you are encountering total strangers. You know nothing of their character and work habits. You have no idea whether the nurse, doctor, or therapist standing before you is conscientious or burned out. Therefore, you need to carefully observe their actions and ask many questions about any dealings that decrease your comfort level. Whenever you suspect that something is awry, trust only your intuition until you receive a satisfactory answer. You may not want to be rude, but do you want to risk a serious infection because someone else is hurrying?

Hazardous Waste

In a hospital, there are many hazardous biological materials. Human excrement and body fluids do not always go down the toilet. Hospital personnel often find feces, urine, blood, mucus, vomit, and bile in the beds and on the furniture and floors. Such substances, if left in place for any length of time, will contaminate the environment. It only takes a minuscule droplet to carry a load of potentially deadly microorganisms to an open wound or to a patient with a weakened immune system. Such droplets are so small that a person would never know that they were on his or her skin. Therefore, the hospital must maintain a quick response program to clean up filth. There must be zero tolerance for any delays. Nurses must immediately cleanse their patients and call housekeeping to wipe down the furniture and the floor with antiseptic solutions. If you experience any waiting after noticing any body waste, you should contact the executive officers. If the situation happens in the evening, on a holiday, or over the weekend, then call the nursing supervisor and complain. If that does not resolve the problem, you can demand that the nursing supervisor page the on-call administrator, who, in turn will call the housekeeping manager. In most hospitals today, department heads have twenty-four-hour responsibility. If no one is cleaning up a biohazard spill, then the housekeeping boss must go to the hospital and get the job done.

Additionally, hospitals must require their personnel to dispose of used needles and syringes in special containers. Since they are only human and sometimes overlook this, you can help yourself or your loved one by checking the bed and the bedside stand for any remaining hazardous waste after each procedure. If you find an exposed needle or some other contaminated device, immediately report it to a nursing supervisor. Do not attempt to discard it yourself. Such an occurrence is a serious incident. If you withhold the report because you want to be "nice," you will prevent the administration from making the responsible person account for his or her negligence.

Isolation of Patients with Infectious Disease

Delays in isolating people with communicable diseases frequently result in an outbreak. However, the timely diagnosis of a disease requiring isolation is mostly a matter of luck. Physicians cannot accurately detect diseases if they are not familiar with the usual symptoms. For example, if there were a new outbreak of measles, the younger doctors might not recognize the symptoms because they have never seen it outside of a textbook. Moreover, many disease carriers display no symptoms, and persons recently infected are going through an incubation period with no indication of being ill. Thus we can only expect doctors and nurses to move infected individuals into isolation as soon as they discover the problem, which could be days or weeks after admission. While you can't always avoid accidental contact with infected persons who have not yet been diagnosed, you will minimize your risks if you simply follow the tips provided in this chapter.

Additionally, certain hospital units house people with suppressed immune systems, such as cancer treatment centers and post–organ transplant floors. Those people are taking drugs that lower their resistance to infection. Also, patients who have very low white blood cell counts from chemotherapy or immunosuppressant drugs must be in reverse isolation because even a common cold virus can be fatal. Therefore, the regulatory and accreditation standards require hospitals to forbid admitting patients with infectious diseases to such units. If you are on such a floor as a patient or visitor, confidentiality rules will prevent you from knowing whether a neighboring patient has an infectious disease. Nonetheless, you can ask the charge nurse every day to assure you that the staff has not breached this life-sustaining policy by placing anyone with an infectious disease on your floor.

Isolation Technique

Keeping people safe from contracting communicable disease requires learning isolation technique. Whether you are a patient or visitor, medical seclusion cannot be effective without your cooperation. See the table on isolation technique beginning on the next page for details on what to do.

As a nursing supervisor, I have often found doctors and nurses in the room of an isolated patient without the required gear. I would hand out the masks and gloves and remind them that they could jeop-

How to Maintain Effective Isolation

Type of Isolation	Required Supplies and Equipment and Patient Restrictions	Instructions
Total—people with diseases that can be spread to others in close proximity or by any contact, such as viral meningitis or SARS; i.e., the individual contaminates the environment	Gown, gloves, hood, and mask. Private room with air-filtration system. Patient must remain isolated at all times. If surgery or scans are necessary, then nurses must arrange to clear the corridors and elevator prior to transport. Transport personnel should also wear sterile protective coverings.	*Entry:* 1. Wash hands thoroughly with antiseptic soap. 2. Don mask, hood, gown, and gloves. *Exit:* 1. Remove gloves without touching gloves to garments or skin. 2. Remove hood, gown, and mask, touching only the inside of these coverings. 3. Dispose of coverings in the red trash can. 4. Wash hands thoroughly with antiseptic soap.
Respiratory—people with contagious respiratory infections such as tuberculosis or viral or penicillin-resistant pneumonia, in which the disease spreads only from respiratory droplets	Gloves and mask. Private room with air-filtration system. The patients must wear a face mask when outside of the room.	*Entry:* 1. Wash hands thoroughly with antiseptic soap. 2. Don mask and gloves. *Exit:* 1. Remove gloves without touching gloves to garments or skin. 2. Remove mask, touching only the edges or string. 3. Dispose of coverings in the red trash can. 4. Wash hands thoroughly with antiseptic soap.

Type of Isolation	Required Supplies and Equipment and Patient Restrictions	Instructions
Contact—people with contagious skin infections such as herpes, impetigo, or staphylococcus infections; also people with infected wounds and gangrene	Gloves and gown. Semiprivate room is okay.	*Entry:* 1. Wash hands thoroughly with antiseptic soap. 2. Don mask and gloves. *Exit:* 1. Remove gloves without touching them to garments or skin. 2. Dispose of coverings in the red trash can. 3. Wash hands thoroughly with antiseptic soap.
Body fluids—standard precautions.	Gloves only. Semiprivate room is okay.	*Entry:* 1. Wash hands thoroughly with antiseptic soap. 2. Don gloves. *Exit:* 1. Remove gloves without touching them to garments or skin. 2. Dispose of gloves in the red trash can. 3. Wash hands thoroughly with antiseptic soap.

(continued on next page)

How to Maintain Effective Isolation *(continued)*

Type of Isolation	Required Supplies and Equipment and Patient Restrictions	Instructions
Reverse isolation— patients with a suppressed immune system and patients in the burn unit.	Protects patient from surrounding environment. Gown, gloves, hood, and mask. Private room with air-filtration system. Patient must remain isolated at all times. If surgery or scans are necessary, then nurses must arrange to clear the corridors and elevator prior to transport. Transport personnel must also wear sterile protective coverings.	*Entry:* 1. Wash hands thoroughly with antiseptic soap. 2. Don mask, hood, gown, and gloves. *Exit:* 1. Remove gloves without touching gloves to garments or skin. 2. Remove hood, gown, and mask, touching only the inside of these coverings. 3. Dispose of coverings in the red trash can. 4. Wash hands thoroughly with antiseptic soap.

ardize the health of other patients as well as their families. Breaches of isolation technique most often go unnoticed, so there should be constant reminders with signs, lapel buttons, and the like. You should speak up, too, for everyone's safety.

Treatment for Infections

The failure to provide appropriate diagnosis and treatment for infection is a common problem. The rules are simple. When there are signs of infection, the doctors are supposed to take cultures before ordering antibiotics. Without the cultures to identify the offending germs, providing treatment is like target shooting while blindfolded. The culture and sensitivity report will tell your doctor which antibiotic to use. In the case of a forty-nine-year-old man with an infected leg wound, the doctor failed to take a culture. Three weeks later the doctor discovered that he had been giving his patient an ineffective antibiotic. By that time the infection had spread to the man's blood and damaged his heart valves.

Sometimes a patient develops a fever of unknown origin. The standard of care for a hospitalized patient is to culture the blood, sputum, and urine and take a chest x-ray. Doctors then should order a broad-spectrum antibiotic pending the culture results, which are usually available within two to three days. If you or a loved one is waiting for a culture and sensitivity report, keep asking for the results every day. You will then need to make certain that the doctor adjusts the antibiotic accordingly.

What You Can Do to Improve the Quality of Health Care

It is not possible to eliminate infection as a complication of hospitalization because the management infrastructure and architectural design actually promotes this raging cluster epidemic. The routine movement of personnel from one patient to another in assembly line fashion lends itself to cross-contamination. Moreover, the broad-based failure to timely diagnose and appropriately treat the newly acquired infections with antibiotics that match the sensitivity test results has compounded the problem. Furthermore, infectious disease consultants and nurse epidemiologists are finding new strains of bacteria that are now resistant to a growing number of antibiotics.

Although scientists have yet to prove this theory, many researchers believe that this is the result of prescribing antibiotics on a large scale without proven sensitivity. Nonetheless, you can make a tremendous difference in reversing this trend if you simply insist that your doctor prescribe only those antibiotics that are proven effective against the particular infection being treated. In some cases, when it is prudent to start treatment before knowing the results of the culture, you should insist that the doctor follow with the culture report as soon as it is available and change the antibiotic if necessary. This is one area of medical treatment where you can prevent doctors and nurses from committing malpractice.

Reducing the Risk of Infection

- Make certain that all personnel wash their hands before touching you or your loved one (see "Cleanliness First").
- Make certain that all personnel put on a new pair of gloves before touching you or your loved one (see "New Gloves for Each Patient").
- Make certain that respiratory personnel are adequate to provide ventilator maintenance with changing of external airway tubes every day (see "Ventilator Maintenance").
- If there is a bladder catheter, make certain that the nurse provides catheter care (see "Caring for Bladder Catheters").
- Speak to the operating room nurse about contamination in the operating room prior to your surgery (see "Operating Room Contamination").
- Observe for breach of sterile technique during dressing changes (see "Dressing Changes").
- Watch for breach of sterile technique during insertion and maintenance of vein catheters (see "Vein Catheter Sterility").
- Look for proper disposal of biohazard waste (see "Hazardous Waste").
- When you or a loved one has to be in isolation, learn what is required (e.g., cap, mask, gown, or gloves) and insist that the nurses and doctors not enter the room unless they follow the same rules (see table entitled "How to Maintain Effective Isolation").
- Make certain that your doctor is prescribing an antibiotic that is going to be effective (see "Treatment for Infections").

10

Dealing with Managed Care: "Your Request for Treatment Has Been Denied"

THERE IS A STORY of a man who hurt his right knee and hobbled to his doctor's office. The receptionist leads the injured man inside and tells him to sit on the examination table. Two men wearing white lab coats, each with a stethoscope around his neck, enter the room. The one whom the patient recognizes as his doctor says to the other, "This is a forty-four-year-old man who fell and hit his knee on the floor while playing racquetball. The MRI shows a torn meniscus. I recommend arthroscopic surgery to repair the cartilage and drain the excess synovial fluid."

"I think not," the second man retorts. "Let us take a more conservative approach. Six weeks of physical therapy and then reevaluate, okay?"

"Yes, sir!" the first man replies as the second man leaves the room.

"Who was that?" the patient asks. "The chief of orthopedics?"

"No, he's the insurance agent."

Every joke has a ring of truth. In this chapter, we will examine how a "league" of health maintenance organizations (HMOs) has taken control of health-care delivery and what we can do to combat unfair denials. As a society, we have been so crushed by the high cost of private insurance that we have unwittingly given corporate executives the authority to veto our doctors' decisions. This veto power seems absolute because the appeals process is toothless. Even though some HMO corporate directors are also medical doctors, the consequences of their decisions relate primarily to money. The irony of this deplorable situation is that sometimes the victim of the profit-driven medical denial and the stockholder motivating that refusal are the same person. In other words, many of us have stock in the very organizations that are limiting our ability to pay for care.

How It All Began

When HMOs first arrived on the scene in the late 1970s, the salespeople touted this as prepaid health care. Their slogan was "You pay us a reasonable fee for future medical services, and we take care of everything." This was supposed to be the answer to holding down spiraling doctors' fees and hospital charges without reducing quality. Doctors and hospitals would share in the monthly revenue from our premiums, and we would have our health-care utopia.

During the first few years, many of the original HMO businesses collapsed. The costs of providing total care exceeded the HMO revenues largely because doctors continued to order an increasing number of prescribed diagnostic tests and high-technology treatments. In response, the insurance industry gave birth to a new corporate enterprise called managed care. The idea was to remove the absolute authority that physicians had enjoyed over their patients' course of treatment in order to keep costs down. They marketed these new plans to employers offering reduced premiums for plans that required members to choose from a network of physicians who had contractually agreed to the plan's terms and conditions. This effort mushroomed over a period of ten years and sprouted hundreds of insurance subsidiaries and independent insurance firms that collectively cut doctors' fees by two-thirds, reduced hospital charges, and made it harder for people to get medical care because most people can't afford to pay privately. The initial reduction of cost drew employers away from the traditional insurance plans, and soon individual health insurance buyers followed suit.

Gradually, the difference between HMO and regular health insurance all but disappeared because the insurance companies bought out the HMOs and converted the product back to insurance while keeping the cost-cutting features of the prepaid health plans. The HMO was originally a company that hired physicians, nurses, and other professionals and directly provided the health care. Now, although a few direct HMO providers still exist, most HMOs have reverted back to being third-party payers that have contracts with self-employed physicians, unaffiliated hospitals, laboratories, and other providers.

As time progressed, the insurance conglomerates, in purchasing the HMOs, became legally qualified as medical service providers and began purchasing hospitals and medical practices. In the reverse, large university-based medical centers bought out many area community hospitals and medical practices and became legally qualified as insurance companies empowered to provide medical services.

Therefore, in today's market, there is much less difference between the insurer and the health-care provider if you are a member of a managed-care health plan. Then again, there seems to be a trend among some of the more successful private physicians to discontinue their membership in HMOs because they no longer want to knuckle under to corporate interference. However, one would have to be confident of maintaining a clientele who can afford to pay large deductibles if not the full cost of his or her services. Unfortunately, most doctors are economically trapped because dropping HMO membership would cause a substantial loss of revenue. The trend toward using HMOs is not likely to be reversed, because a health insurance policy that offers you total freedom of choice with no interference in medical decision will cost about the same amounts in premiums as the HMO, while under the insurance policy, you have to risk paying an additional $6,000 per year if you become sick.

In 1995, when I was a health insurance company executive, I organized a new managed-care division. I gathered large groups of doctors by sending out mailings to every physician in the phone book in a given area. The response rate was about 80 percent from doctors who were begging to join. They wanted to enroll in a provider network list that they knew we would distribute to thousands of members of various unions. These union health plans would only pay for doctors included in the network. This meant that physicians who did not join the network would lose the union customers that they had. We told the eager candidates that the new fee schedule would be 15 percent less than the prevailing Medicare rates (already below market rates), and they still signed up in droves. For most surgical procedures, this was a large reduction. For example, in 1996 we paid an average of $2,300 for an arthroscopy of the knee. The orthopedic surgeons in the New York City area were charging approximately $6,200 in 1994 for the same operation.

Furthermore, as part of the cost containment scheme, we set up precertification. The provider contract required that all the physicians and suppliers were to request prior approval for all elective procedures, therapy, durable medical equipment, and disposable supplies. We had a computer program to assist a group of nurses in making all first-level decisions. We entered the diagnosis code, and the computer program would tell us whether the requested service or item fit the preset criteria. We also created a practice profile of each of the requesting physicians. The directive from the fund managers was to identify those providers whose profile showed the highest medical costs and eventually expel them from the network if they would not alter their methods. Somehow, the physicians knew that they would face a loss of business if they racked up too many prescriptions for high-cost items. Moreover, other companies were structuring their reimbursement schedules to pay primary care physicians a bonus for reducing the number of specialist referrals while penalizing those who increased it.

Regarding the famous rhetoric about maintaining quality, in my own experience my professional staff and I tried to honor our obligation to keep the medical services consistent with our advertised "standard of excellence." Unfortunately, this was self-delusional. We had no way of knowing the clinical performance history of the individual practitioners whom we accepted into the group. We only knew that each of the specialists was board certified and had admitting privileges in at least one of the area hospitals. If any of those doctors had perpetrated a recent string of botched surgeries or had been defendants in malpractice lawsuits, we could not know about it because no one would publicize such data. We only knew that the care would be no worse than what the members were already getting, because most of our customers never had to change doctors or hospitals when we converted their conventional health plans to managed care.

Generally, in spite of the reduced fees and utilization, the cost of the premiums skyrocketed. The monthly membership fee for two adults buying individual plans (not part of a group) aged fifty-four in Florida in the Blue Choice® PPO (preferred provider organization) is $475 if you are willing to risk paying $6,000 out of pocket. The fee is $735 with a $3,000 out-of-pocket risk. This is more than a 300 percent increase in premiums since the managed-care companies took over the health-care industry. Every plan available has some level of deductible or copay, so the original HMO concept of prepaid total health care, with a few exceptions, seems to have vanished.

Although it appears that companies are paying less and charging more, the increase in the cost of premiums results from an increase in total payouts. We called this experience rating. This is a continuing trend because our population is getting older and sicker each year and requires more care. The insurance customers as a whole are paying for those who became ill last year because the law allows insurance companies to pass their losses on to their customers.

The Reality of HMOs Today

By now, HMOs have gained a firm chokehold on most of our medical resources and are fast moving toward total ownership. About two-thirds of the insurance companies have pulled out of the health-care market, with the remaining few engaged in government-sanctioned price fixing and restraint of trade. Most hospitals and medical groups have collectively formed or become part of an HMO conglomerate. This is true of both proprietary and not-for-profit organizations. The federal and state governments have even placed Medicaid and Medicare into corporate hands by paying managed-care companies to accept recipients as members. While it is still voluntary, the government bureaucracies are leaning toward mandatory privatization of all Medicaid and Medicare programs. The U.S. Congress has even passed a law prohibiting lawsuits against managed-care companies and their employees for damages resulting from delayed or denied coverage for necessary diagnosis and treatment. Thus the HMO medical directors can arbitrarily deny expensive medical care, and the victim has no legal recourse other than to file an appeal with the state insurance department unless there is a breach of contract. By the time they complete that lengthy process, it is usually too late. In our multibillion-dollar health-care industry, free enterprise has given way to regional monopolies.

A Cautionary Story

The following story is true except that the names have been changed. It is typical of cases in which doctors want to try treatments that are not yet considered mainstream but that do offer hope for patients.

In April of 1999, when I was a marketing consultant for the Diapulse Corporation of America, an attending internist, Dr. Chadra, of a hospital-based medical clinic, ordered the Diapulse Wound Treatment System for Mary Kaye, a sixty-eight-year-old Jamaican-born female.* She had two pressure ulcers on the outer aspect of her right leg. They were at stage II, which was full-thickness skin loss with

---

* I should mention at this point that I have in the past worked for the Diapulse Corporation of America in marketing their product, and I have received compensation for setting up successful wound-healing programs on hundreds of patients at various health-care institutions and in people's homes. As of this writing, I no longer have any affiliation with the company, and I am not a stockholder. I do not expect to gain financially from mentioning the machine in this book. Also, the management at Diapulse has never asked me to write about their product, and I have not received nor do I expect to receive any compensation for doing so. I fully intend to use this device again under physician's orders in providing wound care should the opportunity arise.

exposure of fatty tissue. The causes of the ulcers were poor circulation, with the leg pressing against the side of the wheelchair where
she spent most of her day. She had suffered a severe stroke two years
earlier. After reviewing multiple reports in various medical journals,
Dr. Chadra learned that many medical researchers had reported success in healing such wounds, thus avoiding amputation.

Dr. Chadra called me, as the equipment vendor and independent
nurse-consultant for wound care, to come to the clinic to see Mrs.
Kaye. I examined her wounds and took several digital photographs
to send to the HMO with the doctor's request for precertification.
We did not anticipate a problem because the HMO had included Diapulse in the network of medical equipment vendors. There was a contract between the two companies. The doctor wrote the prescription
and letter of medical necessity and sent it to the medical review
department. Several days went by and we had not received any
response. Dr. Chadra called Dr. Stein, the medical director of the
HMO, and asked for the approval. Dr. Stein said she had heard of
Diapulse before but she had no knowledge of its effectiveness. Dr.
Chadra suggested that Dr. Stein speak to me for more information.

Within a few days, I was speaking to Dr. Stein on the phone. She
said she needed more information about the Diapulse technology. I
gave her reprints of six research studies published within the previous ten years, all showing the same conclusive results—that all of the
Diapulse-treated ulcers healed.

Dr. Stein then said she wanted Mrs. Kaye to go to a vascular surgeon to rule out arterial obstruction. Dr. Chadra tried to explain that
Mrs. Kaye had already seen a vascular surgeon six months earlier and
that there was no arterial obstruction. However, this did not make
any difference to the medical director. Consequently, Mrs. Kaye saw
the vascular surgeon after waiting two weeks for her appointment.
The diagnosis remained the same. Her condition was inoperable.

Two weeks after receiving the vascular surgeon's opinion that surgery would not improve the circulation, Dr. Stein called and asked
me to take another set of pictures to see if the wounds had gotten
any worse with conventional treatment. More than thirty days had
passed since we made the initial request. When I arrived at Mary

Kaye's home, I found that her condition had deteriorated. The two wounds had gotten worse with exposed muscle and bone, and there was a large stage IV ulceration of her right heel. The left leg had also developed two wounds in the calf area at the stage II level, and all the ulcers were infected. I took the new set of pictures and hand delivered them to Dr. Stein because I was so concerned.

"Doctor, you can see from the wounds that her condition has deteriorated. If we do not treat her soon, she is going to lose first her right leg and then the other."

"Well, it is obvious that she is headed toward amputation. But we still have no assurance that your Diapulse machine is going to make any difference."

"Since you know there is no risk to the patient, don't you believe it is worth trying if there is any reasonable chance of saving her legs?"

"If I were the treating physician I would agree. However, I am not. My job is to evaluate whether the use of Diapulse is worth the financial risk with a chance of saving money. Obviously, it would be much cheaper to use Diapulse than to amputate. But if it turns out that we have to pay for an amputation after paying for Diapulse, then my job is on the line."

"Please give this woman a chance to save her legs."

"I have to discuss this in committee. We will let the member know of our decision. You are merely the equipment vendor, so I will not get into any further discussion with you. Thank you for the information you provided."

One week later, Mrs. Kaye received a denial letter. About thirty days following that, Dr. Chadra called and said that Mary Kaye was in the hospital scheduled for amputation of the right leg in ten days. "The family wants to know if you could bring the Diapulse machine into the hospital."

"I could, but we will need an order and I will have to get administrative approval."

"I am not following the case now. The medical attending is Dr. Rubinsky."

I visited Dr. Rubinsky. He said he had never heard of this machine before, but after looking at the brochure and the medical journal articles, he said, "I am not familiar with this technology. However, I can see that there is no risk of harming the patient. If there is any possibility of avoiding or reducing the amputation, we are obliged to offer it to Mrs. Kaye." He then called the nurses' station on the floor where Mary Kaye was staying and ordered the treatment three times per day for thirty minutes each.

The next day, I was attempting to deliver the Diapulse machine at the hospital when my cell phone rang. It was Dr. Stein. She sounded upset. "Tom, you tried to outflank me with the Diapulse machine, didn't you?"

"Look, Dr. Stein, Dr. Rubinsky called me and wanted to use it on Mrs. Kaye for ten days to try to save her leg. Since she was in the hospital, I did not think that I was required to notify you. This is a deal with the hospital."

"The purchasing director called me to request approval for special reimbursement. You really want to sell your machine pretty badly, don't you?"

At this point, I told her that my commission was 20 percent. For ten days, that came to $150. I offered to waive my commission and discount the price by that amount. I just wanted to give this poor woman one last chance to save her leg.

Dr. Stein said to me, "At this late stage, I don't see any hope for your machine being of any use. I am going to deny payment."

"There is certainly less chance than there would have been if you had said yes two months ago. I think I shall offer the hospital a free rental."

"You can do that, but don't be shocked when you find out that Dr. Rubinsky canceled his order."

"Why are you so determined to chop off this woman's legs? Are you so attached to being right?"

"I am not going to discuss this with you anymore."

After Dr. Stein hung up on me, I went directly to Dr. Rubinsky's office. His receptionist told me that he had canceled the order and he would talk to me about it if I wanted to wait. He kept me waiting for three hours until he finished seeing his last patient. When he finally invited me into his office, I could barely talk. "Why would you do this to that poor woman?"

"Look, Mr. Sharon. You are a nice man, so full of compassion. So, I will be honest. Dr. Stein called me. First she said, 'How could you order a machine that you know nothing about?' I told her that I read the literature that you gave me and that there was no risk of any harmful effect, so there was no harm in trying. I was determined. Then she hit me where it hurts."

"Did she threaten your livelihood?"

"If you repeat this to anyone, I'll deny it. Yes, she did. She reminded me that 70 percent of my patients are members of her Medicare HMO. She did not have to spell it out for me. I canceled the order."

Dr. Rubinsky buckled under the threat of losing 70 percent of his practice. He probably convinced himself that the machine would never have worked. Nevertheless, he will never know if it could have worked, and he will always have a nagging doubt. I, too, could not guarantee anyone that Mrs. Kaye's leg would have been saved by the machine. But it certainly seemed worth a try.

I called Mrs. Kaye's daughter and told her what had happened. She still had the opportunity to threaten to sue the doctors if they did not allow her mother to have access to a risk-free possibility of saving her leg. The patient had a right to know that this technology was available and that other patients in the past with similar conditions had enjoyed a successful outcome. I have not heard from the patient or her daughter since that time, so I don't know whether they took any legal action.

In conclusion, there is no easy answer when an insurance bureaucrat decides to obstruct your physician's medical practice, but unless you get angry and get active, you will not get the treatment that your doctor prescribed. If you are willing to fight some battles for a righteous cause, you can also contact your state assembly member, your congressional representative, and the local news media. If you are fighting against injustice, you will find among them several pairs of sympathetic ears.

If you find yourself or a loved one in a similar position of denied care, don't simply accept the judgment. You may not win every time, but you certainly won't win if you don't try. Following are some steps to follow.

INSIDER TIPS

How to Deal with HMO Denials

- Call the medical director and tell him or her why you need the treatment.
- Submit a letter to ask for an appeal. (The HMO is required to supply you with complete information on how to file an internal appeal and how to file an appeal with the appropriate state agency.)
- Pay for treatment out of pocket if you are able and seek reimbursement.
- If all else fails, consult an attorney.

11

How to Communicate with Hospital Staff to Get Better Service

PEOPLE INTERACT IN a special way in hospitals. Doctors, nurses, therapists, other staff members, and patients come together with all the excess baggage of their lives. Add to that the stress of the environment and the patients' feelings of fear, anxiety, pain, anger, frustration, grief, and altered self-image, and you can see why hospitals sometimes seem like a cauldron of human emotion and frailty. These emotions cause breakdowns in communication because they interfere with listening. Therefore, the focus of this chapter is to learn how to improve communication and thereby improve the quality of your care.

How to Get the Staff to Listen to You

Doctors and nurses may seem to be ignoring your complaints because they are sometimes unable to listen. Conversely, patients often do not hear advice or instructions because they are unable to pay attention. This inattention in the communication between patients and hospital personnel contributes to the many disasters that occur.

Most often, we enter into a conversation interested mostly in ourselves. Then we tend to walk away from the interaction making up a memory of what the other person said that is more consistent with what we wanted to hear than with what he or she intended.

Especially when dealing with matters of your health, you need to take responsibility for the recipient's listening. First, you need to avoid language that will prevent listening. Words that threaten self-esteem or cause embarrassment evoke anger and prevent the other person from giving you a fair hearing. So use neutral words as much as possible.

Second, you need to preface negative comments with words that provide a buffer. It gives the recipient an opportunity to prepare to listen and avoid the reflexive defense of anger and resentment. For example, let us say you want to tell the doctor to wash his hands in front of you. If you say, "I need to see you wash your hands before you touch me," the doctor is likely to hear, "I do not trust you. I think you're going to give me a disease with your filthy hands." You can avoid a problem by saying, "It's not that I don't trust you, but with so many hospital-acquired infections going around, I would have peace of mind by seeing you wash your hands in front of me." With this approach, you anticipated the doctor's likely reaction and removed it by addressing it up front.

Third, avoid placing blame. Questions that begin with "how" or "why" after an incident are attempts to fix blame and will nearly always evoke defensive behavior that contributes nothing to finding a solution. If you find that the other party begins the conversation in a defensive mode, you will need to derail it and move it to a mode that is more conducive to listening. For example, in the story in Chapter 8, when my mother's head nurse started to explain that the bedsore happened on another floor, he thought that I was looking to blame someone. That is why I stopped him by saying that I was interested only in implementing a treatment and prevention plan and was not looking to place blame. In saying that, I was able to refocus the conversation to actions that would accomplish the immediate goal.

The "Crying Wolf" Syndrome

When it comes to hospitals, how we perceive ourselves is not really as important as how the staff perceives us. Accordingly, nurses and doctors will often fail to make a proper assessment because they have developed a preconceived conclusion about a patient. For example, a patient who frequently complains about very minor things actually causes the hospital staff to predetermine that the next complaint will have no merit. This is a dangerous situation that you want to avoid. I call it the "already/always way of thinking."

Back in the early 1980s, a forty-nine-year-old man I'll call Bernard, a former television actor and producer, had become destitute. He survived by faking heart attacks. He would walk into an office-building lobby in midtown Manhattan, grab his chest, and collapse to the floor. The security guard would call 911, and an ambulance would take him to the nearest hospital.

This maneuver guaranteed a bed and three meals per day free of charge, because Bernard never carried any identification and gave fictitious names and addresses. The protocol in those days for a complaint of chest pain in a forty-nine-year-old male was three days in the coronary care unit and two more days in step-down. It took five days to rule out a heart attack.

Bernard made his rounds to every hospital by doing his "act" in different parts of town. When he finally showed up two or three times to the same emergency room with the same paramedics picking him up, they were finally on to his fraud. However, there was no legal recourse. After a while, the emergency room doctors would discharge Bernard from the emergency room as soon as he stepped off the ambulance, believing that he was feigning another heart attack to get free room and board for a few days. They had engaged the "already/always" attitude toward Bernard. His new standard "treatment" became a subway token and directions to the nearest men's shelter.

Bernard finally discontinued his short career as a hospital freeloader and went back to work as an actor. The danger he faced, however, was that if he had suffered a real heart attack during that period, he would not have been able to receive treatment because no one would have believed his symptoms to be real. Lucky for Bernard, that didn't happen.

In another case, two nurses used this already/always way of listening to perpetrate a cover-up in a hospital. Mabel was a seventy-two-year-old woman who was agitated and confused. She screamed at the top of her lungs and shouted obscenities throughout most of the day.

One morning the two nurses went into Mabel's room to transfer her to her bed from a stretcher after returning from a CAT scan. The two nurses put the stretcher next to the bed and forgot to lock the wheels. They told Mabel to scoot over, and she plummeted to the floor between the bed and the gurney. She screamed, complained of hip pain, and yelled, "You two bitches made me fall!"

The two nurses picked Mabel up, put her in the bed, and agreed not to report the incident. They reasoned that since Mabel was screaming and shouting obscenities all the time, no one would pay any attention to her. If there were any injury, no one would discover it for a couple of days. By then no one would be able to determine who was liable.

This scheme actually worked as planned. No one paid any attention to Mabel's complaints of pain because she had unwittingly trained all the staff not to listen to her. It was not until a physical therapist tried to manipulate the leg that he discovered there was something wrong with the hip.

The point of this discussion is for you to be aware that when you enter the hospital as a patient, you create a "public" image. Your main audience is the nursing staff. The nurses will form a behavioral assessment based, in part, on the image that you project. Thus if they see you as a person who would not complain unless something were acutely wrong, the responses to your calls for assistance are likely to be quicker than for those patients perceived to be chronic whiners. Save the complaints for the real problems. Then accept nothing less than quick responses.

Nurse Burnout

Many people have told me that at some point in their lives they ran across a nurse in a hospital who seemed indifferent to human suffering. While investigating malpractice cases I have occasionally come across clear evidence of nurses who demonstrated a wanton disregard of the patient's safety. While such situations are uncommon, the question remains, "How can such a person go to nursing school and spend so many years devoted to caring for other people only to end up being indifferent?" One possible answer is burnout.

We can define burnout as the inability to cope with the continuous stress that a particular job produces. The effects of this phenomenon in the nursing profession should be of special interest to you because when you are in the hospital, the people you most depend on are nurses. The implications are dangerous. Nursing is an occupation that brings on a high level of tension and emotion. Add to that the corporate executives' abuse in creating larger workloads to reduce the cost of operations.

Even though we should always hold individuals accountable for their actions, the hospital managers have to bear some responsibility for creating work environments that add to the emotional stress of dealing with catastrophic trauma, illness, and death. The worst offenders are those who lay off dietary aides, housekeepers, and nursing attendants with the idea that the nurses can perform all the ancillary functions. In many hospitals with budget problems, you will find nurses setting up food trays, emptying garbage cans, and mopping floors on the evening and night shifts in addition to shouldering a full patient load. Moreover, the mass exodus of nurses from the hospital scene increases the workload for those who stay behind. This often leads to being forced to work sixteen-hour shifts with heavier burdens. This type of abuse if unchecked will quickly dampen the enthusiasm toward helping others that all nurses start with.

Although many progressive medical centers have employee assistance programs that offer counseling and group meetings to deal with burnout, you will occasionally come across a nurse who seems curt, rude, or indifferent. It may be burnout, or it may just be an off day, but whether you are the patient or visitor in this instance, you will be stuck with this situation for the duration of that shift. Your understanding of the nurse's undesirable response as a symptom of either a bad day or chronic problem can make a difference in the outcome of your care. Of course, the advice given earlier regarding urgent or emergency problems remains the same. If the nurse is committing malpractice as described, you still need to take appropriate action to obtain the services that you need.

Thus if there is no problem requiring immediate intervention, then you can try talking to the nurse who is responding in a negative way with an opener like "Nursing is tough. I understand that you have a difficult job with a great deal of stress and strain." If this does not change the course of your relationship with this person, then there must be a serious problem with burnout. In that case, you will need to contact a supervisor and insist on changing nurses. Until that happens, you will have to maintain a constant vigil, watching and questioning the nurse's every move. This may exacerbate the nurse's agitation, but your safety or that of your loved one comes first.

Burnout does not come about suddenly. It is a process of deterioration that for nurses usually takes seven years. The warning signs are as follows:

increase in lateness and absences
insubordination with superiors
irritability with colleagues and clients
increase in medication errors
slower responses to call lights
failure to assess changes in clinical condition
making patient observations less frequently
failure to maintain safety
failure to provide routine nursing interventions

The nurse suffering from burnout has lost the ability to care about the results of good work and the consequences of errors and failures. Nurse-managers and their corporate executives are responsible for identifying those who are experiencing such problems and taking reasonable actions to improve performance. If you perceive these problems in a nurse, it's your duty to report your concern to a manager.

The Nurse-Patient Relationship

The scope of nursing as the law defines it goes beyond what the public perceives. Most people see nursing as a task-oriented subservient job, assisting patients with their activities of daily living and providing physician-prescribed medications and treatments. While this is true, it is only part of the picture. The uniform state statute that defines the scope of nursing practice actually empowers nurses to diagnose and treat human responses to existing and potential health problems with such services as health counseling and activities restorative to life and well-being. The only restriction is that a nursing action cannot interfere with or alter an existing medical regimen. This translates to a set of duties and responsibilities that includes the following:

- Take a complete health history upon admission.
- Perform a physical assessment upon admission and at the beginning of each shift.
- Review the medical orders to see that they adequately meet the patient's needs.
- Assess the patient to determine the risk of falling.
- Assess the patient to determine the risk of developing bedsores.
- Conduct an interview for behavioral assessment.
- Assess the patient's relationship with significant others.
- Assess the patient's cultural needs and ability to adjust to hospital environment.
- Assess and document the patient's responses to all medications and treatments.
- Observe for changes in clinical condition.
- Observe for changes in behavior.
- Provide periodic pain level assessment.

- Provide health education to patients and family members.
- Encourage patient to verbalize concerns.
- Advocate for patient in the right to receive competent and appropriate medical treatment.
- Provide first line of defense in responding to life-threatening emergencies.
- Design and implement a nursing care plan that helps the patient to set realistic goals.

The Health History

The nurses have to go beyond taking a mere medical history. They have to get a sense of how you have been living your life, how you react to your environment, and whether you have a personal interest in your health.

The Physical Assessment

The nurses have to check your body from head to toes. This includes listening to your chest and abdomen with a stethoscope. They are even supposed to look in your ears. They also have to give you an opportunity to relate any discomfort or problems associated with any part of your body.

Receiving Orders

The nurses are your advocates. They are supposed to take your side if any doctor's order or action or any hospital policy conflicts with your interests. This means that they are required to use every means possible to protect you from any physical or emotional harm. This also includes any problems that visitors might cause.

Assessing Fall Risk

Nurses must be able to predict with reasonable certainty the likelihood of a patient falling out of bed or from a chair. This ability comes from the experience of knowing what conditions predispose a patient to falling. They derive this information from all the other assessments.

Preventing Bedsores

The nurses must assess the possibility of skin breakdown and take all measures available to maintain skin integrity. When breakdown occurs, they must initiate aggressive wound care.

Knowing the Patient

The nurses have to know about who you are. In order to serve you better, they have to know what scares you, what bothers you, what makes you happy, and how you react to both good and bad news. Additionally, they need to know how you perceive your loss of body functions. They also have to find out what understanding you have of your illness.

Understanding Family Dynamics

The nurses have to understand your relationship with your family members and close friends. They have to know how supportive these people are and whether any of them are willing to take responsibility for your care after you leave the hospital.

Understanding Culture and Lifestyle

The nurses have to identify whether you are going to be able to cooperate with hospital routine. This is when they are supposed to find out your personal preferences and make reasonable accommodations. For example, if the patient is an Orthodox Jewish male, there are certain times of day that he must devote to prayer, and at times he must wear certain items. The nurses must know this at the onset so they can adjust the care plans accordingly. Of course, lifesaving measures take priority.

Assessing Responses to Medications and Treatments

Nurses must know what side effects are possible with your medication and what the symptoms are. They must check you for those possible reactions, and they have to know what to do in case any such effects occur. They must also find out what medications you are allergic to. If you have ever had an allergic reaction to any medications, you should tell the nurse without waiting to be asked.

Observing for Physical Changes and Taking Action When Necessary

Your doctor will usually write orders telling the nurses to notify him or her when certain symptoms appear. In addition to that, the nurses have to use clinical judgment to determine whether there are any unforeseen changes. They must then take immediate action in case of emergency.

Observing for Changes in Behavior

The nurses must observe for changes in mental status or emotional responses. They check for orientation to time, person, and place and observe for changes in affect (facial expression) and body language. They need to have the time to open and carry on a conversation with the patient and explore what they might pick up on as being a potential problem.

Assessing Pain

The nurses need to have time to fill out pain assessment forms. The current standard of care prohibits allowing patients to suffer. If there is an increase of pain or new pain, the nurses must evaluate whether this is symptomatic of a change in clinical condition.

Discharge Planning

Since hospitals are dumping patients while they still need skilled care, most hospitalized people have many things to learn before going home. Some have to learn how to manage diabetes or another chronic disease. Others need to learn how to administer intravenous medications. Still others need to know how to change dressings with sterile technique to avoid infection. In short, nurses have to teach many of their skills to patients and family members, or the discharged patients will develop serious complications while at home. There is also a lot of teaching that nurses have to provide during hospitalization so that their patients will have a better understanding of what is going on.

Encouraging Verbalization of Problems

Nurses must be able to start up a conversation to draw out information that might lead to preventing a serious problem. Some people are stoic and do not like to complain. There are often subtle signs of a potential catastrophe waiting to happen. Again, our nurses need to have the time to perform this important skill.

Advocating for the Patient

At times, patients do not get medical care when needed. Nurses need to stop their routine duties and begin a course of patient advocacy. This involves making telephone calls to page the nursing and medical supervisors. Often in these situations, the nurses have to stay with the patient until management resolves the problem.

Allowing Nurses to Practice Nursing

Whenever an emergency occurs, the nurses are the first responders. If mundane tasks bog them down, they are unable to always be available every time someone stops breathing. There have been too many patients found dead long after it was too late to take action.

The Nursing Care Plan

Nurses have to write a care plan diagnosing every existing and potential health problem with a detailed description of what actions to take and what the goal is. This document sets the standard of care for all subsequent nurses to follow. Moreover, they have to review and revise this care plan every day. I have reviewed numerous hospital charts and have found many instances in which the care plans were missing or had not been updated after the day of admission. Although I do not condone this, I understand it. The nurses' task loads are usually so overwhelming that there is not enough time to practice nursing.

In summary, this long list of time-consuming clinical assessments is a revelation for most people. The most significant defect in the design of hospital structure is that the standard management practices of most hospitals actually impede the nurses and prevent them from giving you the true benefits of nursing care.

Consequently, all new nursing school graduates experience culture shock in making the transition to the hospital because their work assignments do not permit them to practice nursing in accordance with their education. The solution to this dilemma is for hospital managers to hire more ward clerks and nursing attendants. This would give nurses more time to practice nursing. Therefore, if you cannot get your nurse to stop for a few minutes and listen to you, find out if a ward clerk and nurse's aides are working on the floor. If not, you have an issue to take up with the administration. The more time that nurses can spend listening to what you have to say, diagnosing your responses, and planning and supervising your care, the safer your hospital stay will be.

12

Leaving the Hospital Quicker and Sicker

SEVERAL DECADES AGO, doctors controlled when we left the hospital, and people did not usually go home until they were well on their way to recovery. The suitable time to leave the hospital was the result of a discussion between the physician and the patient or a family member. There was no particular motivation to push people out unless there was a shortage of beds.

Today we live in a different reality. Hospitals, being short of cash, have a strong financial incentive to turn the beds over as fast as possible. This new financial incentive comes from the way private and public third-party payers changed the modes of payment. State regulators have adopted two different methods. First, there are the diagnosis-related groupings. This system pays a flat fee for each diagnosis regardless of the length of stay. Admitting two patients consecutively to one bed over ten days brings in twice the revenue as one patient occupying the same bed for the same ten days.

The other method of payment is straight itemized billing for room and board, products, and services on a cost plus basis. This form of revenue also provides a strong financial incentive to turn people over faster because usually about 80 percent of all billable hospital services occur within the first three days. The only difference is that with itemized billing, a low census provides motivation to let people stay a little longer if the beds aren't needed.

The Problems with Early Discharge

During the last twenty years, hospitals' policies have shifted toward earlier discharge because it became financially advantageous to do so. This was not the result of any breakthroughs in medical research. Consequently, people are now going home with all kinds of management problems including the following:

open surgical wounds
unhealed skin grafts
central intravenous lines inserted through the chest wall
central venous lines inserted in the arm
peripheral intravenous lines
limb fractures with external fixators (pins sticking out of
    the legs or arms)
neck fractures with halo splints
unstable pelvic fractures requiring total bed rest

Since doctors and nurses condone such discharges, the question as to whether it is appropriate in any particular case depends on how you feel about you or your loved one going home with conditions that require skilled care. The hospital staff nurses and discharge planners will try to tell you that you have to learn the skills of a registered nurse and accept the responsibility for any complications arising out of making mistakes. This is because the HMOs have decided that if their members take care of themselves, they don't have to pay for as many nursing visits. If you feel up to the task, go for it. If not, you simply have to tell the discharge planner that you refuse to have anything to do with skilled nursing procedures at home. Then the HMOs will be obliged to provide a registered nurse to perform all the required tasks.

Wound Care at Home

Whichever decision you make, you will need to know a few things about the conditions listed in order to make an informed decision. Surgeons usually leave wounds open if there is an infection. The rationale is to allow the purulent material to drain out. The main difficulty here is that the person providing the wound care has to have a strong constitution. Not everyone can handle removing a dressing with foul-smelling drainage and then cleaning out a large gaping hole in some part of the anatomy. You will also need to learn about handling and disposing of contaminated biohazard material without spreading the infection to another part of the body, like the eyes, or to another person.

Going Home with Skin Grafts

Skin grafts that are healing are very delicate. If they get infected or damaged, they are likely to be irreversibly ruined. You will have to be well trained in sterile technique. If the doctor ordered ointments or creams, you will have to apply them very carefully because the slightest injury can destroy the graft.

Going Home with Chest Catheters

People who need long-term intravenous therapy go home with chest catheters. There are several different types of devices, and there is a different method for accessing the line for each one. You will need to be thoroughly familiar with your setup. Ask for the manufacturer's insert. This contains diagrams and instructions. The makers usually provide patient booklets. You should get one if it is available. The recipients of these items are usually people with cancer, AIDS, Lyme disease, or other chronic illnesses who need long-term intravenous feeding, medication, and/or fluids. You must have a registered nurse on call twenty-four hours per day. You can arrange that with a licensed or certified home-care agency.

Going Home with Central Intravenous Lines

Central lines inserted in the arm are percutaneous intravenous catheters (PICs). They are about twenty-four inches long, and many doctors favor them because they are good for long-term use. PICs require meticulous cleansing and dressing changes, with sterile technique, at the insertion site. There is a high risk of infection. This is an alternate choice to chest insertions. With this device also you will need to have a registered nurse on call around the clock.

Going Home with Peripheral Intravenous Lines

Peripheral lines are for short-term use. All of the possible complications discussed in Chapter 5 can occur at home. Again you will need twenty-four hour coverage. Your discharge planner should give you the choice of at least three agencies that have a home intravenous program. Many hospitals have their own agency and will keep out the competition. This is wrong, because competition is one way of getting good service. Moreover, hospitals that deprive you of free choice of vendors are trampling on your rights.

Going Home with an External Fixator

External fixators are tricky. The presence of these devices is a clear indication that the fracture was nasty, with multiple bone fragments. The fixator holds the fragments in place after extensive orthopedic reconstructive surgery. If you neglect the maintenance, the infection will go right down to the bone. This would result in a high risk of gangrene. Thus the pins require meticulous cleaning daily, usually with hydrogen peroxide and saline. I would recommend that most people get a home-care nurse to do this, but if you must do it yourself, learn the proper technique and do not miss any days.

Going Home with a Halo Splint

Regarding neck fractures, once the halo splint is in place, the situation is pretty stable. The only real problem is the awkwardness of this contraption. The patient will need a lot of custodial help with activities of daily living. Additionally, the pins that hold the halo in place are partially screwed into the skull, so you will have to clean them daily with aseptic technique.

Going Home with a Pelvic Fracture

With unstable pelvic fractures or any other condition that requires total bed rest, you are taking home a person who is going to be completely dependent upon a caregiver. Be certain that you and the discharge planner make all necessary arrangements for extra help, or you will be stuck day and night.

The All-Important Discharge Orders

The discharge planner is responsible for making sure that all required equipment and supplies are available to you when you reach home. Therefore, your most important concern is the discharge orders. You will need to review these with the attending physician. If you are in a teaching hospital, the attending physician will probably delegate the discharge process to a resident (doctor-in-training). This is not a problem as long as you make sure that the attending countersigns the orders. You should make certain that the physician you are going to see on the outside is aware of what you need at home. This is an aspect of health care that doctors often overlook. It is going to be up to you to see that this does not happen.

Options to Relatives Providing Care

If you are unsure or feel any apprehension about your new assignment as the family nurse, you have the right to refuse. The discharge planner may talk to you about insurance coverage and may try to tell you that you are going to incur charges at $1,000 per day, but you do not have to give in to coercion. If you take yourself out of the equation, then the hospital owes you a duty to continue providing all the required care. The discharge planner will then have to discuss one of three options with you and your physician: (1) continue hospitalization, (2) transfer to a skilled nursing facility or rehabilitation hospital, or (3) transfer home with full home-care coverage.

In such a situation, there is no standard rule as to which choice is the best one. Your support system, home environment, and financial considerations will be the determining factors. Nonetheless, the hospital is responsible for your well-being regardless of what exists for you at home or in the community. If the hospital cannot guarantee that you will receive everything you need, it is not allowed to discharge you.

However, if the attending physician and discharge planner determine that an intermediate care facility will meet your needs, they can transfer you or charge you private pay rates if you refuse to allow them to move you. Additionally, the choice of discharge options is sometimes a matter of preference or convenience.

For example, when my mother was in the hospital for the fractured right hip, the physicians and discharge planner wanted to send her out on a certain date. The problem was that I had begun renovating her condominium. It needed a complete overhaul because she had not had any work done on it for about twenty years. We needed more time. The social worker said, "We need to transfer your mother to an intermediate care facility."

My mother refused to go because she knew it was just a fancy term for nursing home. I was afraid that such an atmosphere would be psychologically devastating, given that she was already depressed. I only needed ten days more to finish her apartment, after which time I knew she could go to her home with a home attendant.

I got nowhere with the social worker, so I approached the attending rehabilitation doctor and spoke to him about my mother's condition. I reminded him that she had a bedsore and a blood clot in her left leg. He agreed to extend her hospital stay for the additional ten days and then gave me another extension for an additional five. At the end of this final period, Mom's apartment was ready and her equipment, supplies, and home attendant were in place. A simple business negotiation went a long way to avoid subjecting an elderly woman to intense psychological trauma. But I had to be willing to speak up for her.

Inappropriate Discharge and What Happens

Speaking up is very important, as the following stories illustrate.

Esther R. was seventy-six years old when she went into one of the big university medical centers in New York City for a double hip replacement. She went through the surgeries without a hitch. About one week after the operations, the doctors transferred her to the rehabilitation floor. There she went through a series of physical therapies to improve her range of motion. She also had occupational therapy to practice using a commode. After two weeks the rehabilitation team decided it was time for Esther to go home despite limitations in her ability to stand, sit, and walk.

The internal hip prosthesis is a ball joint attached to a shaft made of surgical steel. Steel is harder than bone, especially in the elderly. Therefore, the patient has to be very careful not to exert pressure on the steel shaft because it will break through the wall of the femur. When people sit or squat as one would have to in using the toilet, they exert outward pressure on the steel shaft. The lower they go, the more force there is.

In preparing her to go home, the nurses should have told Esther that she needed a raised toilet seat with armrests to guard against sitting too low when using the toilet and to aid in slowly sitting and rising. The rehabilitation team members should have also recommended that Esther not go home without a home attendant who could assist her with sitting on the commode. No one told her this basic information, and the discharge planners never made any arrangements. In the end, this world-class medical center with a world-renowned rehabilitation department did a wonderful job in replacing the hips and rehabilitating her to functioning level. However, they failed in the process of discharge like most other hospitals. The attending doctor wrote orders for a home-care nurse to evaluate Esther's needs outside of the hospital, and no one responded. The discharge planner should have picked up the order and referred the patient to a home-care agency.

On the day of discharge, Esther went home via ambulette in a wheelchair with her seventy-eight-year-old sister. The equipment vendor delivered a raised toilet seat without armrests. When it was time for Esther to use the toilet, she had no one to help her. Her sister was unable to offer any assistance other than rolling the wheelchair into the bathroom. Esther stood up, turned herself around, and sat down hard on the toilet seat. At that moment she heard a loud cracking noise and felt terrible pain. Her sister at least was able to call 911. The paramedics came, lifted Esther off the toilet, placed her on a stretcher, and brought her back to the medical center. The steel shaft of the hip prosthesis broke through the bone on both sides.

The saddest part of this scenario was that the accident was avoidable. This is true for many accidents. It is simply a matter of doctors, nurses, and therapists giving serious thought to what will happen after a person leaves the hospital. Everyone who took care of Esther either knew or should have known what would happen if she sat too low and/or too quickly. Unfortunately, they did not convey a warning to the patient. If they had, she would have insisted on going home with an attendant.

If you or your loved one is being discharged, be sure that your nurses have evaluated your current health-care needs and anticipated potential health problems and complications.

A few years ago, a social worker at a Manhattan hospital referred Barney, a sixty-eight-year-old man, for ambulette transportation and home care. He had a fractured right femur, which he had sustained when a taxi struck him down while he was crossing the street. The social worker told me that Barney lived on the fifth floor with no elevator. She said he had to leave the next morning, so there would be no time for me to go to the hospital to do a discharge assessment. She also told me that he only needed help in going up the five flights of stairs. So I arranged for an ambulette with two men to bring Barney to his apartment and for a nurse to meet him there to do an in-home assessment.

The next morning I got a call from Barney's next-door neighbor, Robert. "Are you the nurse that is going to take care of Barney? He has your telephone number."

"I have assigned one of my nurses to go see him this evening. Is there a problem?"

"Well, he is sitting on the fifth-floor landing and cannot get into his apartment."

"What is the problem with his apartment? Did he lose his key?"

"No, it's worse than that. There is a lot of debris, and he can't get the door open wide enough to fit the wheelchair."

"Where are the ambulette drivers?"

"They left."

I got in my car and headed downtown to Barney's home. When I got to the fifth-floor landing I went inside his apartment. This was a three-room railroad flat with every room filled to the ceiling with trash. A narrow pathway led to the bedroom, and there was a tiny amount of space in the kitchen for the stove, refrigerator, and table with two chairs. There was also a narrow access path to the bathroom. It was obvious that Barney could not stay there. Besides the fact that he could not fit through the door, we could never get anyone to come in to take care of him. He was in a precarious situation because he could not survive very long in this predicament.

I called Beth, the social worker, to tell her what was happening. "Barney cannot get into his apartment because it is filled with all of his trash from the last twenty-six years. When his wife died, he stopped cleaning house."

Beth became angry. "He never told me anything about that."

"Can I send him back to the hospital?"

"The hospital will not take him back because he has no medical reason to be here."

As flabbergasted as I was, I did not argue because Beth was referring business to me. So I arranged for another ambulette crew to bring Barney to the local YMCA hotel and booked him into a room. Then I got one of my vendor agencies to send a home attendant, who sat with Barney through the night. Afterward I contacted Disaster Masters, a cleaning service company specializing in sifting through mounds of trash, to preserve the valuables and throw away the garbage. Fortunately, Barney had credit cards and some money in the bank, so he was able to pay for everything. If he had been penniless, I would have arranged for him to go to a nursing home after an initial trip back to the hospital emergency room.

So who was at fault here? Certainly Barney would have been better off had he told the whole story. But the social worker did not do an adequate job of assessing Barney's ability to receive care in his home. She blamed him for withholding the facts about his apartment. However, had she engaged him in a detailed discussion about where to put everything and whether the wheelchair would fit through the doors, she would have realized there was a problem.

Between the Cracks

The problem with discharge planning in many hospitals is that management handed over the discharge planning function to social services. This was a huge mistake because the primary skill of social workers is to identify community resources and deal with Medicaid and Medicare eligibility issues. They are not competent to diagnose potential complications arising out of a lack of services, supplies, or equipment. Their primary focus is to move the patient through the door. When corporate executives try to solve their budget problems by assigning duties outside the scope of a particular profession, the result is incompetent performance. And patients are the ones who suffer.

Moreover, many potential problems could result in catastrophic complications when sick, dependent people leave the hospital. While doctors can prescribe the equipment, supplies, and drugs, and social workers can find vendors and identify sources of payment, it is only the nurses who can diagnose potential health problems arising out of unmet needs. Accordingly, the nurses who are best qualified to provide discharge planning services are those with experience in home care. Such nurses would be more familiar with what the patient requires in order to deal with any particular health problem in the home environment.

For a Safer Hospital Discharge

Open surgical wounds

- Do not go home without registered nurse coverage from a licensed or certified home-care agency.
- Do not leave the hospital until you have received all the surgical supplies you will need. One of the treating doctors should write a prescription.
- You have the option to refuse to change the dressing and insist that the home-care agency provide a visiting nurse for daily dressing changes. Self-care is voluntary.
- Make sure that dirty dressing materials are disposed of in plastic bags—do not touch with bare hands.
- Maintain sterile technique with new dressing.
- Be careful not to dislodge any surgical drains. If there is any problem or doubt, call the nurse and/or doctor.
- Observe the wound for foul odor, redness of the surrounding skin, swelling, tenderness, or an increase in pain. Immediately call the nurse and/or doctor if you notice any of these symptoms.

Unhealed skin grafts

- Same instructions apply as for open surgical wounds.
- Be careful not to touch skin graft.
- If you have to apply an ointment or a cream, do so very gently to avoid even the slightest trauma.
- Note the color of the graft. If it gets darker, call the nurse and/or doctor.

Central intravenous lines inserted through the chest wall—single lumen (one tube) or double lumen (two tubes in one)

- Same instructions apply as for open surgical wounds.
- Make sure that the end of the catheter is capped and clamped at all times to prevent hemorrhage.
- Remember that self-care is voluntary.
- Observe the insertion site and immediately call the nurse and/or doctor if you notice any redness, swelling, tenderness, and/or pain.

Central venous lines inserted in the arm (single lumen only)

- The same instructions apply as for central intravenous lines.
- The insertion site must be sealed off with a clear plastic dressing.

Peripheral intravenous lines

- Only a registered nurse with certification may insert a new IV into your vein. And remember that self-care for administration of medications is voluntary.
- The vein catheter must be capped-off and clamped when not in use, with a small amount of anticoagulant inside to prevent clotting.
- If the next intravenous medication is not flowing freely, clamp or close off the line and call the nurse.
- Observe the insertion site and immediately call the nurse and/or doctor if you notice any redness, swelling, tenderness, and/or pain.

Limb fractures with external fixators (pins sticking out of the legs or arms)

- Same instructions apply as for open surgical wounds.
- Keep the pin insertion sites clean and dry with sterile cotton swabs and prescribed solution (doctors usually prefer a mixture of one-half part hydrogen peroxide to one-half part saline).
- Do not allow scab formation at insertion site.
- Observe for signs of infection at pin insertion sites, such as pain, tenderness, redness, swelling, and fever. If you notice any of these, immediately call the nurse and/or doctor.

Neck fractures with halo splints (multiple pins inserted in skull to immobilize the neck)

- Same instructions apply as for open surgical wounds.

Unstable pelvic fractures requiring total bed rest

- Do not go home unless there is a family member or home-care agency able to provide care twenty-four hours per day.
- Do not attempt to get out of bed for any reason.
- Make certain that there is an emergency evacuation plan in case of fire or another emergency.
- You must have the following equipment: electric hospital bed with trapeze, reclining wheelchair, Hoyer lift, bedpan, and urinal (for men).

13

How to Find Out if Your Hospital Is Prepared for Treating Victims of Biological, Chemical, or Nuclear Weapons

SEPTEMBER 11, 2001, was a cataclysmic event that changed everything, including matters in the scope of this book—the standards by which corporate executives must organize and manage their hospitals. The attacks in New York City and Washington, D.C., were a wake-up call. My hospital and all the others had standard disaster plans that we sadly didn't get to use because so few victims lived after the Twin Towers collapsed.

In hindsight, however, many came to realize that the problem was that we were only equipped to handle conventional disasters such as fires, explosions, bus and multiple car collisions, train wrecks, and plane crashes. These types of incidents would usually cause fractures, internal bleeding, head injuries, and burns. It was not a part of our consciousness that the threat of terrorism adds the possibility of infectious epidemics, noxious chemical exposure, and radiation poisoning on a massive scale.

This first attack on U.S. soil since Pearl Harbor was a series of plane crashes aimed at buildings. The surviving victims suffered from injuries that our hospitals were able to handle, and they did a wonderful job. On the other hand, our government and the talking heads on television have been telling us that terrorists will next attack us with biological, chemical, or nuclear weapons of mass destruction.

Accordingly, one of the most important ways that you can prepare for such an eventuality is to know which of your local area hospitals have put out a workable emergency preparedness plan for biological, chemical, and nuclear attacks. This entails calling or visiting the area hospitals and asking the public relations officer a few questions. Therefore, the purpose of this chapter is for you to learn what a hospital needs in order to be prepared to treat large numbers of survivors of biological, chemical, and/or nuclear attack.

While I was writing this book, President Bush signed into law the Office of Homeland Security (OHS). The media says that this is the largest government reorganization since Franklin D. Roosevelt's New Deal. Since the OHS is still evolving, we do not know what its specific function will be in developing new terrorism disaster response plans for hospitals. However, the published OHS bulletin states that there will be many public health and health-care issues to address. Ultimately, there likely will be local branches all over the country. Accordingly, the purpose of this chapter is to assist you in identifying what is missing in your community with regard to saving lives during the aftermath of a terrorist attack.

What Hospitals Need in Order to Treat Biological Attack Victims

Although the media publicity has focused mostly on anthrax because of the contaminated letter attacks in the months following September 11, that is only one of the four best-known biological agents to which the enemy has access. The other three are botulism, bubonic plague, and smallpox.

Anthrax

Anthrax became a bug of interest to terrorists because it is readily available virtually anywhere on this planet. Its scientific name is *Bacillus anthracis*. The natural history of infectious disease from this germ shows that it has been limited to farm animals (mostly sheep and goats) with occasional cross-contamination to human handlers. This infection also carries the name of wool sorter's disease because the most frequent incidences in the United States in recent years have occurred among workers who handled raw sheep's wool or goat hair. Therefore, even when a mere handful of mail sorters and office workers became infected in urban areas, public health professionals immediately knew that this was a deliberate attack.

Since anthrax is an aerobic, spore-forming organism, it is especially dangerous because it thrives in open air, and the spores are like seeds with hard protective shells that a terrorist can spray into the air like fine dust particles. Thus humans can acquire them by inhalation, skin contact, and ingestion (swallowing). When laboratory microbiologists gather large quantities of anthrax spores, it takes on the appearance and consistency of powdered sugar. Hence, it is an ideal material for placement in aerosol cans. Terrorists can set them off like roach-bombs in public places. It would take only a few aerosol bombs in New York's Grand Central Station to infect about one million people during a morning rush hour.

As far as other methods of attack are concerned, we already know that terrorists can use the U.S. mail to send contaminated letters. Additionally, there is also the possibility of contamination of food supplies. Therefore, for your personal protection it is important that you know some more details about anthrax, such as the three different types (pulmonary, cutaneous, and gastrointestinal) and their incubation periods, the common symptoms of each type, and what hospitals need to do to treat and contain the infection. The most dangerous aspect of such an attack is that most people would not become aware of exposure to anthrax until it was too late.

Pulmonary anthrax. With pulmonary anthrax, the spores enter the respiratory system through the nose and lodge in the base of the lungs (alveolar sacs). It only takes one spore to reach the final destination, hatch, and multiply exponentially. Initially, there is an incubation period of one to eight weeks. Following that, the victim gets the same symptoms as the common cold. Two to four days later, there is an abrupt onset of respiratory failure with collapse of the circulatory system. The disease is treatable only if caught during incubation or initial onset of symptoms.

Cutaneous anthrax. The cutaneous form of anthrax disease is a local infection of the skin after direct contact with spores or live bacteria. This usually occurs on the head, forearms, or hands. The symptoms start with itching and a red welt. Then a blister develops, with the skin finally ulcerating with formation of a thick black scab. This is less dangerous than the pulmonary type because there is more time, but treatment is the same. Without treatment, the infection would spread to the blood and become fatal.

Gastrointestinal anthrax. The gastrointestinal form results from swallowing food or liquid contaminated with anthrax spores or bacilli. The food contamination most commonly occurs in meat. The symptoms are abdominal pain, nausea, vomiting, fever, vomiting blood, and bloody diarrhea. The infection usually enters the blood within two to three days after incubation, which takes from one to seven days. This type is usually fatal, with death resulting from septic shock. The only way to get an early confirmation of the diagnosis is a positive stool culture.

Anthrax treatment. The only definitive diagnosis for anthrax is positive blood culture for the pulmonary and gastrointestinal type and positive wound culture of the cutaneous lesion. The treatment of choice after suspected exposure is one of four oral antibiotics given daily for eight weeks:

- ciprofloxacin (Cipro), 500 mg twice daily for adults and 20 to 30 mg per kilogram of body weight per day for children divided into two doses
- levofloxacin, 500 mg once daily for adults only
- ofloxacin, 400 mg twice daily for adults only
- doxycycline (for use if there is an allergy to any of the first three), 100 mg twice daily for adults and 5 mg per kilogram of body weight per day for children divided into two doses

Doctors will order the intravenous form of one these antibiotics if the patient becomes seriously ill.

If someone discovered an empty aerosol bomb in a commuter train station, most of the people who walked through at the time would seek immediate diagnosis and treatment. If this happened in Grand Central Station during one of the rush hours, the surrounding hospitals would have a flood of about one million patients demanding treatment. If as many as three hundred area hospitals were accessible, that would be about thirty-three hundred patients converging on each emergency room within one day. The authorities would have to open up all the convention centers and stadiums, equip them with public showers and a complete change of clothes for each patient, and hand out oral antibiotics like Halloween candy.

Therefore, every hospital needs to have an emergency preparedness plan that specifies how many anthrax exposure victims it can handle at one time. Hospitals should publicize this information so people would know from estimating the size of the attack whether they can expect to get treatment or become part of an angry mob standing in a panic outside the hospital.

Although a terrorist can infect large numbers of people by spraying spores into the air, the good news about anthrax is that there is no true airborne transmission. The spores settle on surfaces like the skin or objects that people normally touch. The infection only occurs from skin contact with a contaminated surface. Therefore, total isolation is not required. The precautions of wearing masks, gowns, and gloves with biohazard disposal are sufficient. The plan for decontaminating new arrivals to minimize the impact of the attack should be as follows:

- Remove patients' clothing slowly and carefully to avoid spreading spores to other surfaces.
- Place clothing in labeled plastic bags.
- Instruct patients to shower thoroughly in provided shower facilities.
- Decontaminate all environmental surfaces with chlorine bleach (one part bleach to nine parts water).

- Instruct personnel to wear full isolation gear (masks, gowns, and gloves) when disposing of contaminated material.

According to the Centers for Disease Control and Prevention, patients should get treatment immediately upon learning that there was a possible anthrax exposure. The ideal course of treatment is to first take blood and/or stool specimens (if there is suspicion of intestinal infection) for culture and prescribe in accordance with the sensitivity report. However, this would become impossible if there was a large-scale exposure.

Accordingly, public health officials must find out how many hospital microbiology laboratories there are in a given city and how many specimens they can process per day. For example, if New York City has 300 such facilities, and each place, given a limited number of technicians and incubators, can handle 200 tests during one crisis, then the local health-care system can confirm only up to 60,000 cases after a single attack that could infect hundreds of thousands.

Another question that officials must answer is whether there are enough antibiotics available to treat the exposed population. If our sample of 60,000 lined up for Cipro, each person would need 112 capsules. The total number required would be 6,720,000. Therefore, a single attack in one railway depot or stadium exposing half a million commuters or spectators would probably wipe out the regional supply of antibiotics before health-care providers could eradicate the infection.

Regarding preventive measures prior to attack, the BioPort Corporation has produced an immunization vaccine for anthrax. Currently, this is routinely available only to military personnel. The official position of the U.S. government is that the risk of anthrax exposure is not great enough to warrant manufacturing sufficient vaccine to inoculate the general population. The fact is that only one company makes the vaccine under contract to the U.S. Department of Defense, and there is not enough to go around. There are limited amounts available for known exposure victims including farmers and veterinarians.

It is important to note that taking antibiotics prior to an attack is unwise because a few hours after the last dose, the protection is gone. People should only take the antibiotics when they have a positive culture or they are reasonably certain that anthrax exposure has occurred.

Botulism

This lethal bacterial by-product disease is rather obscure as a bioterrorism agent. The name of the nasty little culprit is *Clostridium botulinum*. This is also a likely biological weapon because botulinum produces spores that are present in soil and marine sediment throughout the world. Botulism is more difficult to handle in a weapons laboratory because it is anaerobic (it can only thrive in an airless environment).

The most common form of disease in adults is foodborne botulism. Food substances become contaminated and vacuum-packed during manufacturing. The airless environment in cans and bottles allows the culture to grow. Additionally, terrorists have been able to produce large amounts of spores that they could spray into the air and infect people who inhale that air.

Regarding symptoms, the foodborne disease begins with vomiting and diarrhea, and the inhalation form starts with respiratory congestion and coughing. Once a person inhales or ingests the contaminant, the bacterium releases a neurotoxin that causes the following symptoms:

> drooping eyelids
> sagging jaw
> difficulty swallowing
> slurred speech
> blurred vision
> progressive paralysis with the arms first, then the
>   respiratory muscles, and finally the legs
> respiratory failure from muscle paralysis and upper airway
>   obstruction due to the tongue falling backward

This is a horrific condition because there is no loss of sensation or consciousness as the victim slowly suffocates. The listed neurological symptoms begin twelve to thirty-six hours after ingestion and twenty-four to seventy-two hours after inhalation. Therefore, an aerosol attack with botulism spores is likely to result in a much higher death rate than with anthrax.

Botulism treatment. The only known antidote is trivalent botulinum antitoxin, made from horse serum. Each case requires three injections: upon learning of exposure and then at two and twelve weeks after the first injection. There is a 9 percent allergic reaction rate, but doctors can manage that with antihistamines. Additionally, the availability of this lifesaving substance is limited to state health departments and the Centers for Disease Control and Prevention. The only manufacturer in North America that I could find on the Internet is Aventis Pasteur Limited, in Ontario, Canada.

Furthermore, even a small-scale aerosol attack infecting three or four thousand people would cause an acute public health dilemma because virtually every victim, to stay alive, would require an intensive care bed and a respirator for eight to twelve weeks, even after receiving an injection of antitoxin. In New York City, there are approximately six thousand intensive care beds that are usually about 85 percent occupied at all times. That would leave only nine hundred beds (give or take a few dozen) available for an onslaught of several thousand patients with paralytic respiratory failure.

Consequently, your hospital's new disaster plan must have a contingency for alternative makeshift intensive care sites. The health-care providers can utilize any empty warehouse, convention hall, National Guard armory, or other such building with large open space. The plan should also identify inventories of the following items:

hospital beds
hospital linens
mechanical ventilators
crash carts with emergency drugs, syringes, and needles
defibrillators
cardiac monitors

blood pressure monitors
oxygen blood saturation monitors
electrical generators
suction machines
suction catheters
bladder catheters and drainage systems
portable x-ray machines
portable laboratory equipment
ambulance transport with life-support capabilities

Finally, the hospital's new disaster plan should contain procedures for collecting specimens for laboratory diagnosis. In case of attack, the Federal Bureau of Investigation (FBI) is supposed to coordinate the collection and transport of biohazard materials to designated laboratories for diagnostic confirmation. During such an event, public health workers would test only random samplings of victims within various groups. It would not be feasible to test everyone.

Plague

The germ that causes bubonic plague is *Yersinia pestis*. This one almost wiped out everyone in Europe during the Dark and Middle Ages. The natural carriers are fleas that reside on rats. When the rats get into people's homes, the infected fleas jump over to humans and cause blood and lymphatic infections. Since rat control has become a public health priority, this disease rarely occurs today.

But in the hands of the new wave of twenty-first century terrorists, plague bacteria make a formidable weapon. Bioweapon scientists have been able to aerosolize this bug as well and have thereby modified it to an airborne disease. Thus they can artificially produce a pneumonic plague from bubonic plague bacteria. Once this occurs, infected people spread the disease through the air by breathing, talking, sneezing, and coughing. Therefore, one attack would be far reaching because the epidemic would take on a life of its own and literally spread with the wind.

The clinical problems arising from this disease include the following:

fever
cough
chest pain
coughing up blood
cough productive of thick purulent or watery sputum
fluid in the lungs (confirmed on x-ray)

Plague treatment. With regard to management of an exposed population, there is no vaccine available in the United States for pneumonic plague. Accordingly, your hospital executives and public health authorities need to have an operations plan that must include procedures on both decontamination and infection control. Speaking of decontamination, once the aerosolized *Y. pestis* has settled on the skin, clothing, or other personal effects, there is no longer a threat of reintroducing the spores into the air. Nonetheless, there is still a threat of bubonic infection through the skin, so decontamination is imperative. The disaster plan should include the following procedures for all new arrivals when there is reasonable certainty that an attack has occurred:

- Instruct patients to remove all clothing and personal effects and place them in a labeled plastic bag.
- Instruct patients to shower thoroughly using soap.
- Instruct personnel to wear caps, masks, gloves, and gowns when handling contaminated objects.
- Cleanse environmental surfaces with chlorine bleach diluted in water, one part to nine.

Second, regarding control and treatment, since we are dealing with an airborne disease, decontamination will not stop the process of infection if it has already begun. Therefore, health-care workers must isolate all infected individuals. Otherwise, the nurses, doctors, other health-care workers, and rest of the community will also become ill. In addition to the patient being placed in a private room, standard respiratory isolation protocols include personnel wearing head cover, mask, gown, and gloves within three feet of the patient and washing their hands before and after contact.

In case of a terrorist attack, the lack of available private rooms would necessitate placing large numbers of infected people in quarantine. This means placing people together for whom there is a reasonable certainty of recent exposure to the same infective substance. For that reason, the terrorism response plan should have predesignated facilities such as gymnasiums and the other types of large, spacious buildings discussed earlier. Furthermore, one important requirement would be the installation of a ventilation system that could filter out droplets that are as small as five microns in diameter. This kind of effort would also require identifying people in the community who express a willingness to volunteer their services in case such situations arose.

To continue, the treatment of pneumonic or bubonic plague is simple and effective. The first choice is doxycycline, 100 mg twice daily for adults and 5 mg per kilogram of body weight in two doses for children. The second choice is ciprofloxacin (Cipro), 500 mg twice daily for adults and 20 to 30 mg per kilogram of body weight in two doses for children. The treatment should begin as soon as there is a reasonable certainty that exposure has occurred.

Finally, diagnostic confirmation requires positive cultures from blood or sputum. That handling of specimens should be restricted to biosafety level 2 or 3 (BSL-2 or -3) laboratories. Again, the plan should include instructions to contact the FBI (or other designated authority) to coordinate the pickup and processing of specimens for testing.

Smallpox

The culprit responsible for causing smallpox is the variola virus. The reason it is such a dangerous biological weapon is because it has only existed in military laboratories since the late 1960s. Consequently, we have a whole generation of human beings who have never received a vaccine. The threat looms large because some of the few frozen vials that exist are in the hands of certain individuals with hostile intentions.

Smallpox has an insidious onset. During the first two to four days, this disease resembles the flu, with fever and joint and muscle aches. Then the victim breaks out in a rash over the entire body, including the hands and the soles of the feet. One to two weeks later, the rash turns to multiple scabs. The variola is an airborne virus and spreads from person to person via large and small respiratory droplets. Cross-contamination through direct contact can also occur. People with smallpox become contagious at the onset of the rash and remain so for about three weeks until the scabs start to slough.

Smallpox treatment. As with other infectious diseases, health-care workers must have a containment and treatment plan in case there is an exposure to smallpox. First, decontamination procedures are unnecessary.

Second, the only effective treatment available is to vaccinate during the incubation period. The two types of immunizing material are smallpox vaccine (vaccinia virus) and vaccinia immune-globulin (VIG). The vaccine alone is sufficient if the victim receives it within three days of the exposure. If more than three days have elapsed, then the infected person must receive both the vaccine and VIG. The vaccine is now commercially available, and the U.S. Army Medical Research Institute of Infectious Diseases (USAMRIID) holds all available stock of VIG.

Third, the next step is to isolate the infected persons. If there were a large-scale epidemic, quarantine quarters would have to be big enough to house all exposed individuals. Isolation of people with smallpox is difficult. The hospitals will need special equipment. Because of the danger, testing of specimens can only take place in BSL-4 laboratories. Such facilities are only available at USAMRIID. In BSL-4 laboratories, everyone wears spacesuits and oxygen tanks. The smallpox containment protocol would be as follows:

- Install ventilation system with negative air pressure, six to twelve air exchanges per hour, and monitored filtration of air prior to expulsion.
- Wear head cover, gown, and gloves before entering isolation area.

- Wear respirator mask with micro filter for particles less than five microns in width (must meet the minimal National Institute for Occupational Safety and Health standards for particulate respirators).
- Wash hands using antimicrobial agent before and after each contact.
- Limit patient transport as much as possible.

The release of variola virus over even a small area would cause a devastating epidemic. There are not enough facilities available with negative-pressure air-filtration systems to contain this bug. Containment can only happen one of two ways: inoculate everybody or equip several gymnasiums in every city with negative-pressure airflow systems and build thousands of BSL-4 laboratories.

What Hospitals Need in Order to Treat Chemical Attack Victims

The threat of a chemical weapons attack is hanging over us. Chemical warfare has been around for centuries, beginning with the pouring of boiling crude oil on soldiers attempting to invade a fortress or castle. The opposing sides used mustard gas during World War I. The Iraqi government used chemical weapons in their war with Iran and against the Kurdish rebels.

Since we have enemies in our country who want to kill us in large numbers and since it is not difficult to obtain toxic chemicals, it is not a big stretch of the imagination to conclude that we can expect chemical attacks in cities across the country. Either we can live in denial until something happens (heaven forbid) or we can take measures that would save lives.

Noxious chemicals exist in virtually every household in America. If you have any doubts, look in the cabinet beneath your kitchen sink. If a terrorist drives a chemical tanker down "Broadway" or "Main Street" and blows it up (again, heaven forbid), he would be spraying several thousand gallons of lethal gases or liquids all over the town.

What is the emergency response plan for the hospital in your neighborhood?

The two basic components of an appropriate response plan to chemical attack are decontamination and treatment. Decontamination is the first priority because if the chemical agent is still on the skin or clothing, the damaging effects will continue. Additionally, the people providing care would be at risk. Therefore, removing the substance is the only way to stop further damage. Following that, the doctors and nurses can then focus on providing available treatment.

Accordingly, a plan for chemical decontamination should include the following procedures:

1. Set up portable male and female shower areas in the ambulance bay immediately upon activation of disaster protocol.

2. The person in charge of coordinating all services shall designate a decontamination team.

3. The decontamination team shall wear appropriate protective suits and report to the ambulance bay.

4. The triage nurses will screen patients as they arrive to determine priority while a clerk registers them.

5. Patients will disrobe and place their clothes in labeled plastic bags. The decontamination team will assist those who need help.

6. Patients must shower using soap and a soft brush, getting assistance as needed.

7. If the number of patients is too large to decontaminate every one of them in the showers, the fire department must be on hand to open fire hydrants and hose down groups of people using pressure-controlled hoses that would not cause injury.

8. After decontamination, hospital escort personnel will take patients to the designated treatment areas.

Regarding treatment, it would be most helpful to have an understanding of the different types of chemical weapons materials and their effects. Thus in case of exposure, you would be able to avoid panic and calmly make appropriate decisions. There are four different categories of chemical weapons: nerve agents, vesicants, industrial chemicals, and riot-control agents.

First, the commonly known nerve agents are tabun (GA), sarin (GB), soman (GD), and VX. These compounds are pesticides. The Germans developed the G agents during the 1930s, and the British developed the V agents during the 1950s. These are the most toxic of all chemical weapon agents and can cause sudden loss of consciousness, seizures, respiratory failure, and death within minutes. Terrorists can store these neurotoxins in liquid form and transport them in canisters. The G and V agents have different properties. The former are volatile liquids and evaporate quickly while producing toxic vapors. The body absorbs the liquid through the skin and eyes, while the vapors enter through the lungs. VX has a consistency like motor oil and lingers indefinitely on the skin but does not produce a vapor hazard.

Since there would be no time for laboratory diagnosis in the event of chemical attack, doctors would have to diagnose the victims from clinical observation and event history. The nerve agents produce biological effects by inhibiting the producing of the AChE enzyme (acetylcholinesterase). This enzyme controls the levels of acetylcholine, a neurotransmitter (allows impulses to travel between nerve cells). Without this enzyme control, the entire nervous system becomes overstimulated and hypersensitive. The resulting signs and symptoms are as follows:

> increased secretions as in drooling, tearing, runny nose,
> airway congestion, and profuse sweating
> smooth muscle contraction causing pinpoint pupils,
> asthmalike bronchospasms, nausea, vomiting, and
> diarrhea
> skeletal muscle disorder causing spasms, twitching, and
> weakness

central nervous system irritability causing loss of
consciousness, seizure, and respiratory failure
cardiac disturbances causing rapid heart rate, high blood
pressure, and heart block (electrical impulse failure)

Although the media often refers to nerve agents as "nerve gas," this is a misnomer. The "gas" spoken of is vapor. The severity of the exposure depends on the length of time that a person inhales the vapor with the liquid on the skin. A mild exposure will immediately cause eye pain, tearing, blurred vision, runny nose, and asthmatic response (shortness of breath and tightness in the chest). With a moderate dosage, the symptoms will progress to the intestinal tract with nausea, vomiting, and diarrhea. Once the contact becomes severe, the victim will lose consciousness and begin seizing within one to two minutes. After several minutes of nonstop seizure, there is total flaccid paralysis and death. Furthermore, if the amount of nerve agent is large enough in a given attack, the people closest to the source will die within one to two minutes of the strike. With regard to the nerve agents, the German compounds, like sarin, evaporate more quickly than VX. However, VX presents more of a contact hazard, with faster skin penetration.

In view of the foregoing, the planners must bear in mind that the reversibility of nerve agent damages depends on lapsed time from initial exposure to decontamination and treatment. Hospital personnel must go through a series of drills with mock disasters using these new disaster-plan protocols. Everyone has to know exactly where he or she belongs and what his or her job is. Otherwise, the staff would be fumbling around in chaos, with lives being lost as the cost of management failure.

With respect to treatment, three medications are available to treat the signs and symptoms of nerve agent intoxication: atropine, pralidoxime chloride, and diazepam (Valium). The atropine will reverse the symptoms of mild to moderate exposure. Pralidoxime chloride will reverse the chemical processes of sarin and VX. However, this antidote will only work within four to five hours of exposure for sarin and sixty hours of exposure for VX. The Valium will stop the seizure activity but will not change the nature of the nerve agent within the body. The doctors will determine the various dosages.

To continue, the vesicants are sulfur mustard and lewisite. Mustard is both a vapor inhalation and a liquid contact hazard. Regarding mustard, the main problem with this substance is that symptoms usually do not appear until after irreversible damage has occurred. The body absorbs mustard through inhalation or skin contact within one to two minutes, while the lapse of clinical symptoms from exposure to onset is commonly four to eight hours but can happen from two to forty-eight hours. The injurious effects of mustard liquid and vapor are as follows:

> inflammation, swelling, and corneal ulceration of the eyes resulting in blindness
> burning, itching, redness, and blisters of the skin
> nosebleed, sore throat, and hacking cough
> hoarseness of the voice
> shortness of breath and productive cough
> nausea and vomiting
> bone marrow damage resulting in hemophilia and immune deficiency

The amount of permanent harm depends on the dosage or concentration released in a particular attack.

The treatment can only be supportive since there is no known antidote to sulfur mustard exposure. The disaster plan should include protocols for immediate decontamination and certain treatments for the skin, eyes, and airway.

The emergency responders have to decontaminate as quickly as possible by wetting the victim down with a shower or hose. If the mustard is not washed off within thirty minutes of exposure, it will be too late to lessen the effects because the chemical will have been absorbed and the cellular destruction will have already taken place.

For skin that is irritated and itching, any washing and application of any type of soothing lotion would be helpful. Where there are blisters, the required treatment is application of antibiotic ointment and sterile dressings. Additionally, the dressings need changing several times per day with generous rinsing of the wounds.

For the eyes, gentle irrigation would be helpful only within the first few minutes of exposure. Sometimes the eyelids clamp down spastically in response to the chemical assault. When this happens, attempting to force the eyes open would do more harm than good because by this time the damage has already happened. Follow-up treatment usually includes prescribed eyedrops to prevent scarring, antibiotic eye solutions or ointments and petroleum jelly applied to the eyelids to prevent them from being stuck in a closed or open position.

Treatment of the upper airway involves the use of cool mist and cough syrup. Victims with deeper airway effects such as shortness of breath need to be in intensive care with mechanical ventilation support. If there is an asthmatic response, the standard treatment for asthma applies.

Lewisite, although less infamous than sulfur mustard, is a major concern because there are military stockpiles throughout the world. While it produces most of the same effects as mustard, the symptoms appear more quickly before permanent damage occurs. Lewisite also causes more skin injury. Since it causes immediate irritation to the nose and throat, any attempt to run from the exposure would result in deeper lung damage because the breathing would become deeper and more rapid. Additionally, lewisite causes loss of blood volume with injury to the liver and kidneys with no effect on the bone marrow.

Washing the victim with soap and water as quickly as possible will remove most of the chemical and reduce the potential damage. There is an antidote, anti-lewisite, that prevents the shock response with liver and kidney damage.

What Hospitals Need in Order to Treat Nuclear Attack Survivors

The possibility of a terrorist-perpetrated nuclear attack has become a real threat. This has undoubtedly produced various levels of anxiety in all of us. The best way to overcome worry is to trust the Almighty and prepare as best we can. For those who do not survive an attack if it happens, being prepared will obviously not make any difference. For those of us who do survive, a little knowledge will save lives.

With regard to available treatment of and protection against radiation exposure, there are two possible outcomes of a nuclear event: there is no hospital within reach or there is an intact hospital nearby. The former, requiring total self-reliance with home readiness and knowledge of first aid, is beyond the scope of this book. The latter is the focus of this chapter.

The hospital building should be the chief feature of a new disaster plan to prepare for the aftermath of a nuclear attack. First, the planners need to assume that a nuclear blast will likely wipe out communications (including cell phones). Therefore, the hospital should install satellite communication equipment to ensure continuous contact with government authorities, emergency response agencies, and other hospitals.

Second, there is a strong likelihood that there would be no electrical power even if you were a relatively safe distance from ground zero. Every hospital must have electrical generators to provide independent and uninterrupted power. The standard is to have two generators that automatically kick in within thirty seconds of a power outage. Since most such generators are engines running on diesel fuel or gasoline, the important question is, "How long will the current fuel supply last?" Accordingly, the hospital plan also needs to designate a team from the maintenance crew who would look for and identify a source of additional fuel in case of an emergency.

Finally, if you are within driving distance of ground zero, chances are that your hospital is within range of the radioactive fallout. Therefore, it is incumbent upon the hospital executives to plan for sealing off the building and decontaminating the roof and surrounding surfaces, such as the parking lot or garage, walkways, and landscape. The maintenance people would accomplish this with high-pressure hoses. The plan should also call for the cleanup crew to remove the top layer of soil from the unpaved areas. The hospital should also have radioactivity rate meters available to measure radiation.

Recognizing Radiation Sickness

The difficulty with radiation exposure is that symptoms will appear anywhere from a few minutes to twenty years after exposure. The timing depends on the type of radiation, the dosage, and the part of the body exposed. The two basic categories are nonionizing (which is benign) and ionizing (which is harmful). The benign category includes light, radio waves, microwaves, and radar.

Ionizing radiation produces immediate chemical effects on human tissue. The basic types are x-rays, gamma rays, and particle bombardment (neutron beam, electron beam, protons, mesons, and others). Producers of radioactive materials have distributed them throughout the world for a variety of peaceful and military uses, including medical testing and treatment, electrical power, industrial testing, manufacturing, sterilization, submarine power source, and weapons.

Radiation sickness results from exposure to excessive doses of ionizing radiation. Illness-producing exposure can occur from a single large dose (acute) or a series of small doses spread over time (chronic). Acute exposure usually results in illness linked to a characteristic set of symptoms that usually appear in a specific sequence. Chronic exposure usually results in a delayed reaction (often by many years) causing medical problems such as leukemia, other cancers, and premature aging.

The severity of symptoms and illness from radiation depends on the type, the amount, the duration, length of exposure, and the body areas exposed. Symptoms of radiation sickness usually do not occur immediately following exposure. Doctors often use the time lapsed between exposure and onset of symptoms to determine what to expect in terms of severity.

The initial symptoms are nausea, vomiting, diarrhea, and fatigue. The next onset of symptoms may include the following:

headache
shortness of breath
rapid heartbeat
inflammation of the mouth and throat

inflammation of teeth (internally) or gums
hair loss
dry cough
heart inflammation with chest pain
appearance of second- and third-degree burns
permanent skin darkening
multiple bruising all over the skin
hemorrhage
anemia
secondary infection of burn areas

Treatment for Radiation Sickness

There is no antidote to radiation, but symptomatic treatments are available with antinausea drugs, painkillers, and antibiotics. Since radioactive residue would likely be on clothing and skin, decontamination procedures apply the same as with chemical exposure. Decontamination team members should have appropriate protective suits available to carry out their task without danger. Additionally, radiation can cause problems in every organ of the body. Therefore, doctors and nurses have to maintain a vigil with multiple daily monitoring of the blood cell counts, cardiac rhythm, vital signs, and other body functions. When the blood tests confirm immune system compromise, the doctors have to place the victim into reverse isolation.

In conclusion, we have been at war since September 11, 2001. The elusive enemy outside the boundaries of the "Axis of Evil" has no flag or national identity and is loyal only to a perverted religious dogma. Consequently, our government is undergoing a massive reorganization with the establishment and evolution of the Office of Homeland Security. One crucial component of this effort must be the treatment of large numbers of victims.

Accordingly, hospitals have to take on the added responsibility of revising their disaster response plans. Such plans require cooperation with civil defense and police and fire departments in any given community. At this time, it is likely that few hospitals have been able to accomplish this. There is a need for continuing education programs, purchase of capital equipment, and stockpiling of supplies. Most hospitals cannot afford the additional financial burden. Therefore, the OHS needs a division of public health that would set national standards for terrorism disaster response plans, provide continuing education, coordinate mock disaster drills, and provide funding. Since our government leaders have alerted us to the inevitability of a series of large-scale terrorist attacks, the only way we can remain strong as a nation is for every community to be prepared to control the damage and save lives.

14

Accreditation and Risk Management

THERE ARE TWO AREAS of hospital managing that are supposed to give you, the consumer, the best possible chance for a positive hospital experience: accreditation and risk management. Accreditation is a program which, through periodic surveys, seeks to assure that all hospitals operate within acceptable standards and guidelines in meeting patients' needs. Risk management is a function that is supposed to investigate the causes of all undesirable events, promote truthfulness in documentation, and make permanent changes that would prevent such mishaps in the future. Can you as a consumer rely on the decision of the surveyors who declared that your hospital meets the standards of care? Can you be certain that you will receive fair treatment and a straightforward accounting from hospital management once a staff member that you trusted committed negligence? The answers are mixed.

Although most hospital managers pride themselves on getting high marks from accreditation surveyors and most hospitals have quality assurance departments, the hospital environment is often unsafe. Furthermore, risk managers frequently orchestrate the documentation of injurious events to suppress evidence that might be used against the hospital in a lawsuit. Therefore, once you learn the truth about how the corporate executives run their hospitals, you can communicate in a way that will make them more responsive to your needs. Moreover, if you or a loved one becomes injured because of a staff member's carelessness, you can protect your rights by insisting on accurate and truthful documentation.

The Joint Commission Survey and What It Tells You

In most hospitals, when you enter the lobby you will see a large plaque on the wall stating that the facility was "accredited" or "accredited with commendation" by the Joint Commission on Accreditation of Healthcare Organizations. JCAHO is a not-for-profit organization whose members are hospitals, nursing homes, home-care agencies, and in-home surgical supply and medical equipment vendors. The surveyors thoroughly inspect all areas of the health-care facility for environmental safety, cleanliness, documentation, emergency procedures, patient care protocols, and credentialing of professional staff, just to name a few. They also work from a clearly delineated set of standards and rate the hospital as to the percentage of compliance with all the criteria. This system is one of self-regulation and based on the now known fact that accredited hospitals accidentally kill approximately 100,000 and injure about 300,000 people per year, it is an abject failure.

Notwithstanding the sophistication and meticulousness of these surveys, there is one major reason for the gargantuan letdown: in all cases JCAHO notifies the surveyed facilities about three months in advance of the inspection, which occurs once every three years. Therefore, any representation that a JCAHO accreditation assures quality of care is suspect. The accreditation only shows that the facility has been compliant with JCAHO standards for about thirty days before and during the survey once every three years.

Moving forward, the hospital scene during the three-month period prior to the inspection is a flurry of activity, with mock surveys, managers' meetings, staff meetings, and scrambling to provide previously neglected in-service and to update personnel files and patient documentation. The level of management scrutiny and dedication to upholding the highest standards is at its peak during this period, and it is a time of high levels of stress and anxiety, long hours, and fear of job loss. The period that follows is one of celebration for the relief from the stress. Unfortunately, this is followed by the relaxation phase when everything slides back to the "normal" way of doing things, with the supervision becoming much less stringent. In many instances, the usual way of managing is blatantly substandard, with an illusion of propriety displayed for the surveyors during their stay. As soon as the survey is finished, the mirage evaporates.

For example, a hospital in New York City spent about $30 million building a high-tech emergency suite designated as a level I trauma center. The problem was that it was too small to serve the needs of the surrounding community. Consequently, the hospital management adopted a policy of placing two patients in each of the cubicles that were designed for only one. This was being done in violation of JCAHO standards and health department regulations. The CEO issued strict instructions prohibiting the diversion of patients to other facilities because diverting patients is equivalent to diverting revenue.

After a year of this state-of-the-art facility's being continuously operated in the aforesaid substandard mode, JCAHO notified the hospital that the surveyors were coming in ninety days for the accreditation inspection. The management immediately instituted a hospital-wide program of mock surveys, in-service conferences, patient chart review, and examination of the professional credentialing files to bring everything up to standard. Not surprisingly, during the week that the surveyors were on the premises, the emergency department had only one patient per cubicle. This was accomplished by diverting ambulances to other hospitals during peak times and speeding up the process of admitting or discharging patients from the emergency room. In short, the hospital became generally more efficient during the survey with more staff people working overtime. The overcrowding and chaotic ambience resumed as soon as the inspectors were gone because the ambulances were no longer being diverted and the extra overtime was eliminated.

During the survey preparatory period, the hospital's nursing education department hired me as a consultant to review the credentialing files of the emergency department nurses and bring them up to date for the survey. There had not been a nurse educator assigned to the emergency department for almost one year, so it was no surprise that when I started to review the files, I found that more than 50 percent of them were missing one or more requirements. The missing items were continuing education courses and skills evaluations including, in some cases, the basic and advanced life-support certification. In short, about half the nurses in the emergency department were unqualified to work there. Furthermore, the only motivation for updating those files was the JCAHO survey.

I worked feverishly with another educator and the staff nurses to provide classes and testing. The day before the survey, one of ten files still had something missing. The director told me to stay home during the survey because my job was done. Afterward, she told me that the education department got a perfect rating. Somehow, the surveyors never saw the files with missing requirements. Whether that was the result of hiding the incomplete files or just plain luck, I do not know. However, the fact remains that the surveyors never knew about the way in which the education department normally conducted its affairs and that the "perfect score" was undeserved.

Notwithstanding the reality that the system of self-regulation in the hospital and nursing home industry is nothing more than an elaborate charade, the public has the right to hold the health facilities accountable for failure to adhere to the standards promulgated by JCAHO. Such standards include the following:

appropriate skill level of those performing invasive
    procedures
environmental safety
adherence to patients' rights
infection control
prevention of medication errors
prevention of decubitus ulcers
prevention of falls
maintenance of biomedical equipment

emergency supplies on hand
emergency protocols in place
staff knowledge of emergency procedures
response time to patient calls for assistance

This information should be useful as a checklist when having a conversation with a hospital manager about the quality of services that you or a loved one receives. The more knowledge you have about how things are supposed to be, the more responsive those managers will become to your complaints. JCAHO publishes several volumes of standards by which the organization conducts surveys. More information is available at jcaho.org.

Nonetheless, let there be no misunderstanding—it takes a huge amount of effort for a hospital or nursing home to receive a greater than 90 percent compliance rating (as most of them do). Management personnel have to put in long hours and conduct frequent inspections and scrutiny of their staff. Ideally, this is how management should be conducting itself at all times. In fairness, I don't know if it is possible to maintain such a gargantuan effort on a perpetual basis. Managers would burn out, and staff people would be running for the exits. On the other hand, a constant vigil with even a fraction of the vigor found during survey time would save lives.

The State of Risk Management

I recently sat through a hospital orientation program. A man came in and gave a one-hour lecture on his role as a risk manager. His focus was on incidents that resulted in or were likely to result in a lawsuit. He told us about the case of a ten-year-old boy who was growing up with cerebral palsy, which caused severe spastic paralysis over his entire body. The risk manager said, "While I acknowledge that the hospital staff screwed up and contributed to this boy's terrible affliction, it is my job to protect the financial integrity of this institution. So, we are doing what we can to look for ways to defend against the allegations. The upper management decides and I follow orders."

The striking aspect of this comment was that accepting responsibility for wrongdoing had no place in this man's conversation. This
is a microcosm of the corporate culture—one man or woman does
his or her job to the best of his or her ability while the ethical considerations are someone else's responsibility. Middle managers often
pass the morality buck to upper management, who pass it to the
CEO, who in turn passes it to the board of directors or trustees. The
directors or trustees will consider only the financial welfare of the
stockholders or the public trust.

The appropriate focus for a risk manager is to prevent malpractice and accidents, not just lawsuits for such things. The ideal risk
manager will carefully study the common complications and injuries
that take place as a result of being in the hospital and will recommend changes that will prevent such undesirable occurrences. This
activity should begin with investigating events that have already happened and assigning culpability where it belongs. This means also
identifying any mitigating circumstances that contributed to the blun-
der or omission. This utopian risk manager will then submit a report
holding nothing back.

Regrettably, in the real world, risk managers and investigators
must walk within political boundaries. Their investigative goal is to
counsel employees to document problematic events in a way that will
not provide any evidence to the plaintiff in support of a malpractice
claim. The usual advice for filling out an incident report is "Document only what you find. For example, if a patient falls, just say
'patient found on floor.' Describe the injuries, if any, but do not say
anything about how he fell. If there is anything in your observation
that might suggest a cause of the accident like side rails down or slippery stuff on the floor, do not say anything about it. We do not want
you to lie, but we also do not want you to offer any information or
opinions that might help the plaintiff and hurt our defense."

There seem to be two definitions of risk management. One is the
risk of losing money, and the other is the risk of the same type of
accident happening to the same or another patient. Hospital managers do not have to choose between one and the other because if
they prevent further accidents, they will save tons of money. During

the past year, I have reviewed several cases in which the patient fell out of bed or from a chair two or three times, with the permanent or fatal injury arising from the last fall. In each of these scenarios, if the hospital or nursing home management had a risk management program focusing objectively on the cause, the serious injury would have been avoided. Therefore, the hospital's risk management strategies were a factor in producing the injuries.

For example, John B. was a seventy-six-year-old man who went to a local community hospital by ambulance on April 10, 1998, after complaining of chest pain. The admission assessment revealed that while at home, he got up at night to go to the bathroom and fell and sustained some bruising on his left elbow and hip. The medical history revealed that he had mild emphysema with a chronically reduced blood oxygen level. Despite these obvious red flags, the nurses did not do a fall risk assessment, and fall prevention was not a part of the care plan.

On the third night of admission, John wandered out into the hallway at 2 A.M. and fell in front of his doorway. The nurses who witnessed this picked him up and put him back in bed. The charge nurse filled out an incident report and gave it to the nursing supervisor. The supervisor countersigned the report and recorded the incident in the daily nursing office log. She also sent a copy to the risk management department. No one conducted any investigation nor revised the patient's care plan.

Three days later, one of the nurses found John on the floor in his room, unconscious, at 6 A.M. She called for help and put him back to bed with the assistance of two others. Within six hours, John died of a massive brain hemorrhage. An inquiry would have uncovered a serious problem in a lack of real risk management at the bedside level. The root cause of this untimely death happened because the slipshod attitude toward safety started at the top and oozed downward to the staff.

Several doctors and politicians are saying that there are too many medical malpractice lawsuits. The current rhetoric seems to blame personal injury attorneys for this problem, so the plan of attack is to take away the rights of victims to get justice by creating roadblocks in malpractice legal procedure and reducing the maximum contingency fees for the plaintiffs' attorneys.

This argument presupposes that hospital corporate executives, doctors, and nurses are doing the best they can and the casualties are unavoidable. In my view, we need to seek federal legislation that will mandate fiscal responsibility and standards for safe hospital care. This law should also hold people in management positions personally accountable for being negligent.

Under current law, if the state or local health department investigates a patient's death after receiving a complaint and finds gross negligence at the managerial level, the harshest penalty they can impose is a fine. In other words, when a group of executives commits criminal negligence resulting in a person's death, the current government response is to leave the offenders in charge and take money away from an institution that is already strapped for cash rather than charging the responsible parties with a crime or even insisting on their dismissal.

INSIDER TIPS

Preserving Your Rights After an Accident or Careless Mistake

- Contact a lawyer.
- Remain friendly and courteous at all times while in the hospital.
- Get the names of all the nurses and doctors involved in your or your loved one's care.
- Submit a written request for a copy of your hospital record (in most states, hospitals are required by law to comply immediately and free of charge).
- Write down all the details as you know them—do not rely on your memory.
- File a complaint with your state health department and ask for an investigation.

One Final Note

Insider Tips on Protecting Yourself in the Hospital

Keeping a Daily Log

It is best to keep a daily notebook log from the time you enter the hospital until you leave. Write down everything you feel might be important. Here is a suggested format:

Date and Time	Name and Title of Person Entering Room	Action Taken	Comments
2/20/03 8 A.M.	Jane Doe, R.N.	Medication	I asked what the blue pill was for—she told me it was to lower my blood pressure
10 A.M.	John Smith, lab technician	Draw blood for tests	Filled two large tubes. He stuck me three times before finding a vein. My left inner elbow has a bluish lump under the skin where he stuck me. I told the nurse.
11 A.M.	Bill Jones, transport person	To take me to x-ray	The man was rude. He yanked on my right arm to pull me over from the bed to the stretcher and hurt my shoulder. I told the nurse.

Index